HATE SPEECH!

Joan C. Alvin
Reform Publisher

TABLE OF CONTENTS

OLD TESTAMENT

And God spake all these words, saying, I am the LORD thy God, which have brought thee out of the land of Egypt, out of the house of bondage. (1) **Thou shalt have *no* other gods before me.** (2) **Thou shalt *not* make unto thee any graven image,** or any likeness of any thing that is in heaven above, or that is in the earth beneath, or that is in the water under the earth. <u>Thou shalt not bow down thyself to them, nor serve them</u>: **for I the LORD thy God am a *jealous* God, visiting the INIQUITY of the fathers upon the children unto the third and fourth generation of them that <u>H-A-T-E</u> me;** ***And shewing mercy unto thousands of them that love me, and KEEP MY COMMANDMENTS.*** (3) **Thou shalt *not* take the name of the LORD thy God in vain;** for the LORD will *not* hold him guiltless that taketh his name in vain. (4) **Remember the sabbath day, to keep it holy.** Six days shalt thou labour, and do all thy work: But the SEVENTH DAY is the sabbath of the LORD thy God: in it thou shalt not do *any* work, thou, nor thy son, nor thy daughter, thy manservant, nor thy maidservant, nor thy cattle, nor thy stranger that is within thy gates: For in six days the LORD made heaven and earth, the sea, and all that in them is, and rested the SEVENTH DAY: wherefore the LORD *blessed* the sabbath day, and hallowed it. (5) **Honour thy father and thy mother:** that thy days may be long upon the land which the LORD thy God giveth thee. (6) **Thou shalt *not* kill.** (7) **Thou shalt *not* commit adultery.** (8) **Thou shalt *not* steal.** (9) **Thou shalt *not* bear false witness against thy neighbour.** (10) **Thou shalt *not* covet** thy neighbour's house, thou shalt not covet thy neighbour's wife, nor his manservant, nor his maidservant, nor his ox, nor his ass, nor any thing that is thy neighbour's. And all the people saw the thunderings, and the lightnings, and the noise of the trumpet, and the mountain smoking: and when the people saw it, they removed, and stood afar off. And they said unto Moses, Speak *thou* with us, and we will hear: but let not God speak with us, **lest we die.** And Moses said unto the people, FEAR NOT: *for* GOD IS COME TO **PROVE** YOU, **and that his fear may be before your faces,** THAT YE SIN NOT. (Exodus 20:1-20)

And the LORD spake unto Moses, saying, Speak unto all the congregation of the children of Israel, and say unto them, YE SHALL BE HOLY: *for* I THE LORD YOUR GOD AM HOLY. **Ye shall *fear* every man his mother, and his father, *and* KEEP MY SABBATHS: I am the LORD your God. Turn ye not unto idols, nor make to yourselves molten gods:** I am the LORD your God. And if ye offer a SACRIFICE OF PEACE OFFERINGS unto the LORD, YE SHALL OFFER IT AT YOUR OWN WILL. It shall be eaten the same day ye offer it, and on the morrow: and if ought remain until the third day, it shall be burnt in the fire. And if it be eaten at all on the third day, it is ABOMINABLE; it shall *not* be accepted. Therefore every one that eateth it shall bear his INIQUITY, *because* he hath *profaned* the hallowed thing of the LORD: and that soul shall be cut off from among his people. **And**

4

when ye reap the harvest of your land, thou shalt not wholly reap the corners of thy field, neither shalt thou gather the gleanings of thy harvest. And thou shalt not glean thy vineyard, neither shalt thou gather every grape of thy vineyard; thou shalt leave them for the poor and stranger: I am the LORD your God. YE SHALL NOT STEAL, **neither deal falsely,** NEITHER LIE ONE TO ANOTHER. **And ye shall not swear by** *my* **name falsely, neither shalt thou profane the name of thy God:** I am the LORD. THOU SHALT NOT DEFRAUD THY NEIGHBOUR, NEITHER ROB HIM: **the wages of him that is hired shall not abide with thee all night until the morning.** THOU SHALT NOT CURSE THE DEAF, NOR PUT A STUMBLINGBLOCK BEFORE THE BLIND, **but shalt** *fear* **thy God: I am the LORD.** YE SHALL DO NO UNRIGHTEOUSNESS IN JUDGMENT: **thou shalt not respect the person of the poor, nor honor the person of the mighty:** but in righteousness shalt thou judge thy neighbour. THOU SHALT NOT GO UP AND DOWN AS A TALEBEARER among thy people: **neither shalt thou stand against the blood of thy neighbour;** I am the LORD. THOU SHALT NOT **HATE** THY BROTHER IN THINE HEART: thou shalt in any wise rebuke thy neighbour, and *not* suffer sin upon him. **Thou shalt not avenge, nor bear any grudge against the children of thy people,** *but* THOU SHALT LOVE THY NEIGHBOUR AS THYSELF: I am the LORD. **Ye shall keep my statutes.** THOU SHALT NOT LET THY CATTLE GENDER WITH A DIVERSE KIND: **thou shalt** *not* **sow thy field with mingled seed:** *neither* SHALL A GARMENT MINGLED OF LINEN AND WOOLLEN COME UPON THEE. **And**

5

whosoever lieth carnally with a woman, that is a bondmaid, betrothed to an husband, and not at all redeemed, nor freedom given her; she shall be SCOURGED; they shall not be put to death, because she was not free. *And* HE SHALL BRING HIS TRESPASS OFFERING UNTO THE LORD, unto the door of the tabernacle of the congregation, even a ram for a trespass offering. And the priest shall make an atonement for him with the ram of the trespass offering before the LORD for his sin which he hath done: *and the sin which he hath done shall be forgiven him.* And when ye shall come into the land, and shall have planted all manner of trees for food, then ye shall count the fruit thereof as *un*circumcised: **three years shall it be as *un*circumcised unto you: it shall *not* be eaten of.** But in the fourth year all the fruit thereof shall be holy to praise the LORD withal. And in the fifth year shall ye eat of the fruit thereof, that it may yield unto you the increase thereof: I am the LORD your God. YE SHALL NOT EAT ANY THING WITH THE BLOOD: **neither shall ye use enchantment, nor observe times.** YE SHALL NOT ROUND THE CORNERS OF YOUR HEADS, neither shalt thou mar the corners of thy beard. **Ye shall not make any cuttings in your flesh for the dead,** NOR PRINT ANY MARKS UPON YOU: I am the LORD. **Do not prostitute thy daughter, to cause her to be a whore;** lest the land fall to whoredom, and the land become full of wickedness. YE SHALL KEEP MY SABBATHS, *and* REVERENCE MY SANCTUARY: I am the LORD. **Regard not them that have familiar spirits, neither seek after wizards,** to be defiled by them: I am the LORD your God. THOU SHALT RISE UP BEFORE THE HOARY HEAD, and

HONOUR THE FACE OF THE OLD MAN, and FEAR THY GOD: I am the LORD. **And if a stranger sojourn with thee in your land, ye shall not vex him.** *But the stranger that dwelleth with you shall be unto you as* <u>one born among you</u>, *and* <u>thou shalt love him as thyself</u>*; for ye* were strangers in the land of Egypt: I am the LORD your God. YE SHALL DO NO UNRIGHTEOUSNESS IN JUDGMENT, in meteyard, in weight, or in measure. Just balances, just weights, a just ephah, and a just hin, shall ye have: I am the LORD your God, which brought you out of the land of Egypt. *Therefore* SHALL YE OBSERVE ALL MY STATUTES, and ALL MY JUDGMENTS, and "DO" THEM: I AM THE LORD. (Leviticus 19:1-37)

Ye shall therefore keep *all* my statutes, and *all* my judgments, and "DO" them: that the land, whither I bring you to dwell therein, spue you *not* out. And ye shall *not* walk (live) in the manners of THE NATION, which I cast out before you: for they committed all these things, and therefore **I <u>ABHORRED</u> THEM.** But I have said unto you, Ye shall inherit their land, and I will give it unto you to possess it, a land that floweth with milk and honey: I am the LORD your God, ***which have separated you from other people.*** YE SHALL THEREFORE PUT DIFFERENCE BETWEEN **CLEAN BEASTS** and <u>UNCLEAN</u>, and **BETWEEN UNCLEAN FOWLS** and <u>CLEAN</u>: *and* ye shall not make your souls **a-b-o-m-i-n-a-b-l-e** by beast, or by fowl, or by any manner of living thing <u>that creepeth on the ground</u>, **which I have separated from you as UNCLEAN.** ***And ye shall be HOLY unto me: for I the LORD am holy, and***

7

have SEVERED you from other people, that ye should be MINE. A man also or woman that hath a FAMILIAR SPIRIT, or that is a WIZARD, **shall surely be put to death:** they shall stone them with stones: their blood shall be upon them. (Leviticus 20:22-27)

And I set my tabernacle among you: and my soul shall n-o-t <u>abhor</u> you. *And I will walk among you, and will be your God, and ye shall be my people.* I am the LORD your God, which brought you forth out of the land of Egypt, that ye should not be their bondmen; and I have broken the bands of your yoke, and made you go upright. *B-u-t* **IF YE WILL N-O-T HEARKEN UNTO ME,** *and* **WILL N-O-T DO ALL THESE COMMANDMENTS;** *and* **IF YE SHALL <u>DESPISE</u> MY STATUTES,** *or* **IF YOU SHOULD <u>ABHOR</u> MY JUDGMENTS, SO THAT YE WILL N-O-T DO ALL MY COMMANDMENTS,** *but* **THAT YE BREAK MY COVENANT:** *And* **IF YE SHALL <u>D-E-S-P-I-S-E</u> MY STATUTES,** *or* **IF YOUR SOUL <u>A-B-H-O-R</u> MY JUDGMENTS, so that ye will not do** *all* **my commandments, but that ye break my covenant: <u>-I also will do this unto you</u>; I will even appoint over you <u>terror</u>, <u>consumption</u>, and the <u>burning ague</u>, that shall <u>consume the eyes</u>, and cause <u>sorrow of heart</u>: and ye shall <u>sow your seed in vain</u>, for your enemies shall eat it. And I will <u>set my face against you</u>, and ye shall be <u>slain before your enemies</u>: <u>they that HATE you shall reign over you</u>; and <u>ye shall flee</u> when none pursueth you. And** *if* **<u>ye will not yet for all this hearken unto me</u>,** *then* **<u>I WILL PUNISH YOU S-E-V-E-N TIMES MORE FOR YOUR SINS</u>.**

And I will break the pride of your power; and I will make your heaven as iron, and your earth as brass: And your strength shall be spent in vain: for your land shall not yield her increase, neither shall the trees of the land yield their fruits. And *if* ye walk contrary unto me, and will not hearken unto me; I WILL BRING S-E-V-E-N TIMES MORE PLAGUES UPON YOU ACCORDING TO YOUR SINS. (Leviticus 26:11-21)

A-n-d i-f

YE WILL *NOT* FOR ALL THIS HEARKEN UNTO ME,

b-u-t

WALK CONTRARY UNTO ME;

T-h-e-n

I WILL WALK CONTRARY UNTO

Y-O-U A-L-S-O

IN F-U-R-Y;

and I, even I, WILL CHASTISE you S-E-V-E-N TIMES for your sins. And ye shall eat the flesh of your sons, *and* the flesh of your daughters shall ye eat. *And* I will destroy your high places, and cut down your images, *and* cast your carcases upon the carcases of your idols, *and* MY SOUL SHALL A-B-H-O-R YOU. *And* I will make your cities waste, *and* bring your

9

sanctuaries unto desolation, *and* **I will not smell the savour of your sweet odours.** *And* **I will bring the land into desolation***: and* **your enemies which dwell therein shall be astonished at it.** *And* **I will scatter you among the heathen,** *and* **will draw out a sword after you***: and* **your land shall be desolate,** *and* **your cities waste.** *T-h-e-n shall the land enjoy her SABBATHS, as long as it lieth desolate, and ye be in your enemies' land; even then shall the land rest, and enjoy her SABBATHS. As long as it lieth desolate it shall rest;* **because** IT DID NOT REST IN YOUR SABBATHS, WHEN YE DWELT UPON IT. (Leviticus 26:27-35)

If **they shall confess their INIQUITY,** and the INIQUITY of their fathers, with their TRESPASS which THEY TRESPASSED AGAINST ME, and that also they have WALKED CONTRARY UNTO ME; And that

"I" ALSO HAVE WALKED

CONTRARY UNTO "THEM,"

and

HAVE BROUGHT THEM INTO THE LAND OF THEIR ENEMIES;

if **then their uncircumcised hearts be humbled, and they then ACCEPT OF THE PUNISHMENT OF THEIR INIQUITY:** *Then* will I remember my covenant with Jacob, and also my covenant with Isaac, and also my covenant with Abraham will I remember; and I will remember the land. The land also shall be left of them, and shall enjoy her SABBATHS, while she lieth desolate without them: *and* **they shall accept of the PUNISHMENT OF THEIR INIQUITY:** *because,* **even** *because* **THEY <u>D-E-S-P-I-S-E-D</u> <u>MY</u> <u>JUDGMENTS</u>, and because THEIR SOUL <u>A-B-H-O-R-R-E-D</u> <u>MY</u> <u>STATUTES</u>.** *And yet* for all that, when they be in the land of their enemies, *I will <u>not</u> cast them away, <u>neither</u> will I <u>**A-B-H-O-R**</u> them, to destroy them utterly, and to break my covenant with them:* for I am the Lord their God. *But* <u>I will for their sakes remember the covenant of their ancestors</u>, whom I brought forth out of the land of Egypt in the sight of the heathen, that I might be their God: I am the LORD. These are the statutes and judgments and laws, which the LORD made between him and the children of Israel in mount Sinai by the hand of Moses. (Leviticus 26:40-46)

And it came to pass, when the ark set forward, that Moses said, *Rise up, LORD, and let thine enemies be scattered; and* **let them that <u>HATE</u> thee** *flee* **before thee.** (Numbers 10:35)

And say thou unto the people, Sanctify yourselves against to morrow, and ye shall eat flesh: for ye have wept in the ears of the LORD, saying, Who shall give us flesh to eat? for it was well with us in Egypt: therefore the LORD will give you flesh, and ye shall eat. Ye shall not eat one day, nor two days, nor five days, neither ten days, nor twenty days; But even **A WHOLE MONTH, <u>until it come out at your nostrils, and it be LOATHSOME unto you</u>:** *because* **that YE HAVE <u>D-E-S-P-I-S-E-D</u>**

THE LORD the LORD which is among you, and have wept before him, saying, Why came we forth out of Egypt? (Numbers 11:18-20)

But your little ones, which ye said should be a prey, them will I bring in, and *they* shall know THE LAND WHICH YE HAVE **D-E-S-P-I-S-E-D**. *But* **as for you, your carcases, they shall fall in this wilderness.** And your children shall **wander** in the wilderness forty years, and bear *your* whoredoms, until *your* carcases be wasted in the wilderness. After the number of the days in which ye searched the land, even forty days, **each day for a year,** shall ye bear **your iniquities,** even forty years, and *ye shall know my BREACH OF PROMISE.* I the LORD have said, **I will surely do it unto all this EVIL congregation, that are gathered together** *against* **me: in this wilderness they shall be CONSUMED, and there they shall DIE.** And the men, which Moses sent to search the land, who returned, and made all the congregation to **murmur** against him, by bringing up a **slander upon the land,** Even those men that did bring up **the evil report upon the land, DIED BY THE PLAGUE BEFORE THE LORD.** (Numbers 14:31-36)

Ye shall have one law for him that sinneth through *ignorance,* both for him that is born among the children of Israel, and for the stranger that sojourneth among them. *But* **the soul that DOETH OUGHT PRESUMPTUOUSLY, whether he be born in the land, or a stranger, the same reproacheth the LORD; and that soul shall be CUT OFF from among his people.** *Because* **HE HATH D-E-S-P-I-S-E-D THE WORD OF THE LORD, and HATH BROKEN HIS**

12

COMMANDMENT, that soul shall utterly be CUT OFF; his iniquity shall be upon him. (Numbers 15:29-31)

And Moses called all Israel, and said unto them, Hear, O Israel, the statutes and judgments which I speak in your ears this day, that ye may learn them, and keep, and do them. *The LORD our God made a covenant with us in <u>Horeb.</u>* The LORD made not this covenant with our fathers, but with US, EVEN US, who are all of us here alive this day. The LORD talked with you FACE TO FACE in the mount out of the midst of the FIRE, (I stood between the LORD and you at that time, to shew you the word of the LORD: for ye were afraid by reason of the fire, and went not up into the mount;) saying, *I am the LORD thy God, which brought thee out of the land of Egypt, from the house of bondage.* (1) **<u>Thou shalt have none other gods before me.</u>** (2) **<u>Thou shalt not make thee any graven image,</u>** or any likeness of any thing that is in heaven above, or that is in the earth beneath, or that is in the waters beneath the earth: Thou shalt not bow down thyself unto them, nor serve them: **for I the LORD thy God am a JEALOUS God, visiting the INIQUITY of the fathers upon the children unto the third and fourth generation of them that <u>H-A-T-E</u> me,** *And shewing mercy unto thousands of them that love me and keep my commandments.* (3) **<u>Thou shalt *not* take the name of the LORD thy God in vain</u>: for the LORD will *not* hold him guiltless that taketh his name in vain.** (4) **<u>Keep the SABBATH day to sanctify it,</u>** as the LORD thy God hath commanded thee. Six days thou shalt labour, and do all thy work: But the SEVENTH DAY is the SABBATH of the LORD thy God: in it thou shalt not do *any* work, thou, nor thy son, nor thy daughter, nor thy manservant, nor thy maidservant, nor thine ox, nor thine ass, nor any of thy cattle, nor thy stranger that is within thy gates; that thy manservant and thy maidservant may rest as well as thou. And remember that thou wast a servant in the land of Egypt, and that the LORD thy God brought thee out thence through a mighty hand and by a stretched out arm: *therefore the LORD thy God* **commanded** *thee to KEEP THE SABBATH DAY.* (5) **Honour thy father and thy mother,** as the LORD thy God hath commanded thee; that thy days may be prolonged, and that it may go well with thee, in the land which the LORD thy God giveth thee. (6) **Thou shalt not kill.** (7) **Neither shalt thou commit adultery.** (8) **Neither shalt thou steal.** (9) **Neither shalt thou bear false witness against thy neighbour.** (10) **Neither shalt thou desire thy neighbour's wife,** neither shalt thou covet thy neighbour's house, his field, or his manservant, or his maidservant, his ox, or his ass, or any thing that is thy neighbour's. These words the LORD spake unto all your assembly in the mount out of the midst of the fire, of the cloud, and of the thick darkness, with a great voice: and he added no more. And he wrote them in TWO TABLES OF STONE, and delivered them unto me. (Deuteronomy 5:1-22)

For thou art an HOLY PEOPLE unto the LORD thy God: the LORD thy God hath chosen thee to be a SPECIAL PEOPLE unto himself, above all people that are upon the face of the earth. The LORD did **not** set his love upon you, nor choose you, because ye were more in number than any people; for <u>ye were the fewest of all people</u>: *But because the LORD <u>loved you,</u> and because he would <u>keep the</u>*

oath *which he had sworn unto your fathers,* hath the LORD brought you out with a mighty hand, and redeemed you out of the house of bondmen, from the hand of Pharaoh king of Egypt. *Know therefore that the LORD thy God, HE IS GOD, the faithful God, which keepeth covenant and mercy with them that LOVE HIM and KEEP HIS COMMANDMENTS to a thousand generations;*

And

r-e-p-a-y-e-t-h them that H-A-T-E him

TO THEIR FACE,

to *d-e-s-t-r-o-y* them:

he will *not* be slack to him that H-A-T-E-T-H him,

he *will* r-e-p-a-y him TO HIS FACE.

Thou shalt *therefore* KEEP THE COMMANDMENTS, and THE STATUTES, and THE JUDGMENTS, which I command thee this day, to DO them. Wherefore it shall come to pass, *if* ye hearken to these judgments, and keep, and do them, that the LORD thy God shall keep unto thee the covenant and the mercy which *he* sware unto thy fathers: *And* he will love thee, and bless thee, and multiply thee: he will also bless the fruit of thy womb, and the fruit of thy land, thy corn, and thy wine, and thine oil, the increase of thy kine (cattle), and the flocks of thy sheep, in the land which he sware unto thy fathers to give thee. *Thou shalt be blessed above all people:* there shall not be male or female barren among you, or among your cattle.

And the LORD will take away from thee all sickness, and will put none of the evil diseases of Egypt, which thou knowest, upon thee; *but* **will lay them upon all them that H-A-T-E** *thee.* And thou shalt consume all the people which the LORD thy God shall deliver thee; thine eye shall have NO pity upon them: *neither* shalt thou serve their gods; for that will be a SNARE unto thee. (Deuteronomy 7:6-16)

The graven images of their gods shall ye BURN with fire: thou shalt not desire the silver or gold that is on them, nor take it unto thee, lest thou be SNARED therein: for it is an ABOMINATION to the LORD thy God. Neither shalt thou bring an ABOMINATION into thine house, lest *thou* be a CURSED thing *like it:* **but thou shalt** *u-t-t-e-r-l-y* **D-E-T-E-S-T it,** *and* **thou shalt** *u-t-t-e-r-l-y* **A-B-H-O-R it; for it is a CURSED thing.** (Deuteronomy 7:25-26)

Observe and hear ALL these words which I command thee, *that it may go well with thee, and with thy children after thee for ever,* when thou doest that which is GOOD and RIGHT in the sight of the LORD thy God. When the LORD thy God shall CUT OFF the nations from before thee, whither thou goest to possess them, and thou succeedest them, and dwellest in their land; TAKE HEED to thyself that thou be not snared by following them, after that they be destroyed from before thee; and that thou enquire not after their gods, saying, **How did these nations serve their gods? EVEN SO WILL I DO LIKEWISE.** Thou shalt *not* do so unto the LORD thy God: for *e-v-e-r-y* ABOMINATION to the LORD, WHICH HE

H-A-T-E-T-H, have they done unto their gods; **for even their SONS and their DAUGHTERS they have BURNT IN THE FIRE to their gods.** What thing soever I command you, observe to do it: thou shalt not add thereto, nor diminish from it. (Deuteronomy 12:28-32)

That which is altogether JUST shalt thou follow, that thou mayest live, and inherit the land which the LORD thy God giveth thee. Thou shalt *not* plant thee a grove of any trees near unto the altar of the LORD thy God, which thou shalt make thee. *Neither* shalt thou set thee up *any* IMAGE; **which the LORD thy God H-A-T-E-T-H.** (Deuteronomy 16:20-22)

And it shall come to pass, when ALL these things are come upon thee, ***the blessing*** *and* **the curse,** which I have set before thee, and thou shalt CALL THEM TO MIND among all the nations, whither the LORD thy God hath driven thee, And shalt RETURN unto the LORD thy God, and shalt OBEY his voice according to *all* that I command thee this day, thou and thy children, WITH ALL THINE HEART, and WITH ALL THY SOUL; That *t-h-e-n* the LORD thy God will turn thy captivity, and have compassion upon thee, and will return and gather thee from all the nations, whither the LORD thy God hath scattered thee. *If* any of thine be driven out unto the outmost parts of heaven, from thence will the LORD thy God gather thee, and from thence will he fetch thee: And the LORD thy God will bring thee into the land which thy fathers possessed, and thou shalt possess it; *and he will do thee good,* and multiply thee above thy fathers. And the LORD thy God will CIRCUMCISE THINE H-E-A-R-T, and

17

the HEART OF THY SEED, *to love the* L**ORD** *thy God with all thine heart, and with all thy soul, that thou mayest live.* **And the** L**ORD** **thy God will put all these CURSES upon thine enemies, and on them that H-A-T-E thee, which PERSECUTED thee.** And thou shalt RETURN and OBEY the voice of the L**ORD**, and do *all* his commandments which I command thee this day. And the L**ORD** thy God will make thee plenteous in every work of thine hand, in the fruit of thy body, and in the fruit of thy cattle, and in the fruit of thy land, for good: *for the* L**ORD** *will again rejoice over thee for g-o-o-d,* as he rejoiced over thy fathers: *If* thou shalt hearken unto the voice of the L**ORD** thy God, to keep his commandments and his statutes which are written in this book of the law, *and if* thou turn unto the L**ORD** thy God with *all* thine heart, and with *all* thy soul. For this commandment which I command thee this day, it is *not* hidden from thee, neither is it far off. It is *not* in heaven, that thou shouldest say, Who shall go up for us to heaven, and bring it unto us, that we may hear it, and do it? Neither is it beyond the sea, that thou shouldest say, Who shall go over the sea for us, and bring it unto us, that we may hear it, and do it? *But the word is very nigh unto thee, in thy mouth, and in thy heart, that thou mayest DO it.* ***SEE, I HAVE SET BEFORE THEE THIS DAY LIFE and GOOD, and* DEATH and EVIL;** *In that I* **command** *thee this day to love the* L**ORD** *thy God, to walk in his ways, and to keep his commandments and his statutes and his judgments,* ***that thou mayest live and multiply:*** *and the* L**ORD** *thy God shall bless thee in the land whither thou goest to possess it.* ***B-u-t if* thine heart turn away, so that thou wilt not hear, but shalt be drawn away, and worship other gods,** and <u>serve them</u>; I denounce unto you this day, that **YE SHALL SURELY PERISH,** and that ye shall **not** prolong your days upon the land, whither thou passest over Jordan to go to possess it. I call heaven and earth to record this day against you, that I HAVE SET BEFORE YOU **LIFE and DEATH, BLESSING and CURSING:** *therefore <u>CHOOSE LIFE</u>, THAT BOTH THOU and THY SEED MAY LIVE:* **That thou mayest** *love* **the** L ORD **thy God, and that thou mayest** *obey* **his voice, and that thou mayest** *cleave* **unto him:** *for HE IS THY LIFE,* **and the length of thy days:** that thou mayest dwell in the land which the L ORD sware unto thy fathers, to Abraham, to Isaac, and to Jacob, to give them. (Deuteronomy 30:1-20)

They *p-r-o-v-o-k-e-d* **him to JEALOUSY with strange gods, with** *a-b-o-m-i-n-a-t-i-o-n-s* **provoked they him to ANGER. <u>They sacrificed unto devils,</u>** <u>*not*</u> to God; to gods whom they knew not, to new gods that came newly up, whom your fathers feared not. Of the Rock that begat thee thou art unmindful, and **hast <u>FORGOTTEN GOD that formed thee</u>.** And when the L ORD saw it, **HE A-B-H-O-R-R-E-D THEM,** *because* of the p-r-o-v-o-k-i-n-g of his <u>sons</u>, and of his <u>daughters</u>. And he said, **<u>I will hide my face from them</u>, <u>I will see what their END shall be</u>:** *for* they are a **very FROWARD generation,** children in whom is **no faith. They have moved me to JEALOUSY with that which is not God; they have** *p-r-o-v-o-k-e-d* **me to ANGER with their vanities: and I will move them to JEALOUSY with those which are not a people;** *"I"* **will provoke** *"them"* **to anger with a foolish nation.** *For* **A FIRE IS KINDLED IN MINE ANGER, and SHALL BURN UNTO**

THE L-O-W-E-S-T   H-E-L-L, *and shall* c-o-n-s-u-m-e the earth with her increase, and set on fire the foundations of the mountains.   **I will HEAP mischiefs upon them; I will spend mine <u>arrows</u> upon them.**   **They shall be burnt with <u>hunger</u>, and <u>devoured</u> with burning heat, and with bitter <u>destruction</u>: I will also send the <u>teeth of beasts</u> upon them, with the <u>poison of serpents</u> of the dust.**   **The <u>sword without</u>, and <u>terror within</u>, shall <u>destroy</u> both the young man and the virgin, the suckling also with the man of gray hairs.**   I said, I would scatter them into corners, I would make the remembrance of them to *cease* from among men: Were it not that I feared the wrath of the enemy, lest their adversaries should behave themselves strangely, and lest they should say, Our hand is high, and the LORD hath not done all this.   For they are A NATION VOID OF COUNSEL, *neither* IS THERE ANY UNDERSTANDING IN THEM.   **O that they were WISE, that they understood this, that they would CONSIDER THEIR LATTER END!**   (Deuteronomy 32:16-29)

FOR THE LORD SHALL JUDGE HIS PEOPLE, and REPENT HIMSELF FOR HIS SERVANTS, when he seeth that **their power is gone,** and there is none shut up, or left.   And he shall say, <u>Where are their gods, their rock in whom they trusted,</u>   Which did eat the fat of their sacrifices, and drank the wine of their drink offerings? let *them* rise up and help you, and be your protection.   See now that I, EVEN I, AM HE, and there is no god with me: **<u>I kill, and I make alive</u>; <u>I wound, and I heal</u>:** *neither* **is there any that can deliver out of my hand.   For I lift up my hand to heaven, and say, I live for ever.   If I whet my glittering sword, and mine hand** take hold on judgment; I WILL RENDER V-E-N-G-E-A-N-C-E TO MINE ENEMIES, and WILL REWARD THEM THAT H-A-T-E ME. I will make mine arrows drunk with blood, and my sword shall devour flesh; and that with the blood of the slain and of the captives, from the beginning of REVENGES UPON THE ENEMY. *Rejoice, O ye nations, with his people: for he will AVENGE the blood of his servants, and will render VENGEANCE to his adversaries, and will be **merciful** unto his land, and to his people.* (Deuteronomy 32:36-43)

They shall teach Jacob thy judgments, and Israel thy law: they shall put incense before thee, and whole burnt sacrifice upon thine altar. Bless, LORD, his substance, and accept the work of his hands; **smite through the loins of them that rise against him, and of them that H-A-T-E him, that they rise *not* again.** (Deuteronomy 33:10-11)

Wherefore the sin of the young men was VERY GREAT before the LORD: **for men A-B-H-O-R-R-E-D the offering of the LORD.** (1 Samuel 2:17)

Wherefore the LORD God of Israel saith, I said indeed that thy house, and the house of thy father, should walk before me for ever: *but* now the LORD saith, Be it far from me; *for them that honour me I will honour,* and **THEY THAT D-E-S-P-I-S-E ME SHALL BE LIGHTLY ESTEEMED.** (1 Samuel 2:30)

And the LORD sent Nathan unto David. And he came unto him, and said unto him, There were two men in one city; the one rich, and the other poor.

The *rich* man had exceeding many flocks and herds: But the *poor* man had nothing, save one little ewe lamb, which he had bought and nourished up: and it grew up together with him, and with his children; it did eat of his own meat, and drank of his own cup, and lay in his bosom, and was unto him as a daughter.   And there came a traveller unto the rich man, and he spared to take of his own flock and of his own herd, to dress for the wayfaring man that was come unto him; but took the poor man's lamb, and dressed it for the man that was come to him.   <u>And David's anger was greatly kindled against the man</u>; and he said to Nathan, **As the LORD liveth, the man that hath done this thing shall surely DIE: And he shall restore the lamb F-O-U-R-F-O-L-D, because he did this thing, *and* because he had NO PITY.**   And Nathan said to David, **T-H-O-U <u>ART</u> <u>THE</u> <u>MAN</u>.** Thus saith the LORD God of Israel, I anointed thee king over Israel, and I delivered thee out of the hand of Saul;   And I gave thee thy master's house, and thy master's wives into thy bosom, and gave thee the house of Israel and of Judah; and if that had been too little, I would moreover have given unto thee such and such things. *Wherefore* **HAST THOU <u>D-E-S-P-I-S-E-D</u> THE COMMANDMENT OF THE LORD, TO DO EVIL IN HIS SIGHT?** thou hast killed Uriah the Hittite with the sword, and hast taken his wife to be thy wife, and hast slain him with the sword of the children of Ammon.   ***Now therefore* <u>the sword</u> <u>shall never depart from thine house</u>;** *because* **THOU HAST <u>D-E-S-P-I-S-E-D</u> ME,** and hast taken the wife of Uriah the Hittite to be thy wife.   Thus saith the LORD, ***Behold,* I WILL RAISE UP EVIL AGAINST THEE OUT OF THINE O-W-N HOUSE,** and I will take thy wives before thine eyes, and give them unto thy neighbour, and he shall lie with thy wives in the sight of this sun. For thou didst it SECRETLY: *b-u-t "I"* WILL DO THIS THING **BEFORE** ALL ISRAEL, and **BEFORE** THE SUN. And David said unto Nathan, **I HAVE SINNED AGAINST THE LORD.** And Nathan said unto David, *The LORD also hath put away thy sin; thou shalt not die. H-o-w-b-e-i-t, because* **BY THIS DEED THOU HAST GIVEN GREAT OCCASION TO THE ENEMIES OF THE LORD TO B-L-A-S-P-H-E-M-E, the child also that is born unto thee shall surely DIE.** And Nathan departed unto his house. And the LORD struck the child that Uriah's wife bare unto David, and it was very sick. (2 Samuel 12:1-15)

And the LORD God of their fathers sent to them by his messengers, rising up betimes, and sending; *because he had compassion on his people, and on his dwelling place: B-u-t* they **MOCKED** the messengers of God, and **D-E-S-P-I-S-E-D** his words, and **MISUSED his prophets,** *u-n-t-i-l* THE WRATH OF THE LORD AROSE AGAINST HIS PEOPLE, till there was **no remedy.** (2 Chronicles 36:15-16)

Behold, *HAPPY IS THE MAN WHOM GOD CORRECTETH: therefore* **D-E-S-P-I-S-E N-O-T THOU THE CHASTENING OF THE ALMIGHTY:** *For* **he maketh sore, and bindeth up: he woundeth, and his hands make whole.** He shall deliver thee in SIX troubles: yea, in SEVEN there shall no evil touch thee. In (1) **famine** he shall redeem thee from death: and in (2) **war** from the power of the sword. Thou shalt be hid from the (3) **scourge of the tongue:** neither shalt thou be afraid of (4) **destruction when it cometh**. At destruction and (5) **famine thou shalt laugh**: neither shalt thou be afraid of the (6) **beasts of the earth**. For thou shalt be in league with the stones of the field: and the beasts of the field shall be at peace with thee. And thou shalt know that thy tabernacle shall be in peace; and thou shalt visit thy habitation, and shalt *not* sin. Thou shalt know also that thy seed shall be great, and thine offspring as the grass of the earth. Thou shalt come to thy grave in a full age, like as a shock of corn cometh in in his season. Lo this, we have searched it, so it is; HEAR IT, and KNOW THOU IT FOR THY GOOD. (Job 5:17-27)

Give ear to my words, O LORD, consider my meditation. Hearken unto the voice of my cry, my King, and my God: for unto thee will I pray. *My voice shalt thou hear in the morning, O LORD; in the morning will I direct my prayer unto thee, and will look up.* **For thou art *not* a God that hath pleasure in WICKEDNESS: *neither* shall EVIL dwell with thee. The FOOLISH shall *not* stand in thy sight: thou H-A-T-E-S-T *all* workers of INIQUITY. Thou shalt DESTROY them that speak LEASING (lies): the LORD will A-B-H-O-R the BLOODY *and* DECEITFUL man.** *But as for me,* I will come into thy house in the multitude of thy mercy: and in thy fear will I worship toward thy holy temple. Lead me, O LORD, in thy righteousness because of mine enemies; make thy way straight before my face. **For there is *no* faithfulness in their mouth; their *inward* part is very wickedness; their throat is an open sepulchre; they flatter with their tongue. DESTROY TOU THEM, O GOD;** let them fall by their *own* counsels; cast them out in the multitude of their transgressions; *for* **they have REBELLED against thee.** *B-u-t let all those that put their trust in thee* <u>*rejoice:*</u> *let them ever* <u>*shout for joy,*</u> **because** *thou defendest them: let them also that love thy name be* <u>*joyful*</u> *in thee. For thou,* LORD, *wilt bless the* **righteous;** *with favour wilt thou compass him as with a shield.* (Psalm 5:1-12)

Why standest thou afar off, O LORD? why hidest thou thyself in times of trouble? **The WICKED in his PRIDE doth <u>persecute the poor</u>: let them be** *taken* **in the devices that they have imagined. For the WICKED <u>boasteth of his heart's desire,</u> and <u>blesseth the covetous,</u> WHOM THE LORD A-B-H-O-R-R-E-T-H.** The wicked, through the **PRIDE of his countenance, <u>will** *not* **seek after God: God is** *not* **in ALL his thoughts.</u> <u>His ways are** *always* **grievous</u>; thy judgments are far above out of his sight: as for all his enemies, <u>he puffeth at them</u>.** He hath said in his heart, <u>**I shall not be moved:** for **I shall never be in adversity.**</u> **His mouth is full of <u>cursing** *and* **deceit** *and* **fraud:</u> under his tongue is <u>mischief** *and* **vanity</u>.** **He sitteth in the <u>lurking</u> places of the villages: in the <u>secret places doth he murder the innocent</u>: his <u>eyes are privily set against the poor</u>.** **He lieth in <u>wait secretly</u> as a lion in his den: <u>he lieth in wait to catch the poor</u>: he doth catch the poor, when he draweth him into his net. <u>He croucheth, and humbleth himself</u>, that the poor may fall by his strong ones.** **He hath said in his heart, GOD HATH FORGOTTEN: HE HIDETH HIS FACE; HE WILL NEVER SEE IT.** (Psalm 10:1-11)

In the LORD *put I my trust:* how say ye to my soul, Flee as a bird to your mountain? **For, lo, the wicked bend their bow, they make ready their arrow upon the string, <u>that they may privily shoot at the UPRIGHT IN HEART</u>.** If the foundations be destroyed, what can the righteous do? The LORD is in his holy temple, the LORD's throne is in heaven: HIS EYES BEHOLD, HIS EYELIDS T-R-Y, THE CHILDREN OF MEN. THE LORD T-R-I-E-T-H THE RIGHTEOUS: ***b-u-t* the WICKED and him that LOVETH VIOLENCE his soul <u>H-A-T-E-T-H</u>. Upon the wicked he shall rain <u>snares</u>, <u>fire</u> and <u>brimstone</u>, and an *h-o-r-r-i-b-l-e* <u>tempest</u>: this shall be the portion of their cup.** *For the righteous* LORD *loveth righteousness; his countenance doth behold the upright.* (Psalm 11:1-7)

The king shall joy in *thy* strength, O LORD; and in *thy* salvation how greatly shall he rejoice! *<u>Thou hast given him his heart's desire, and hast not withholden the request of his lips.</u>* Selah. For thou preventest him with the *blessings of goodness:* thou settest a crown of pure gold on his head. <u>He asked life of thee, and thou gavest it him, even length of days for ever and ever</u>. His glory is great in thy salvation: honour and majesty hast thou laid upon him. For thou hast made him most blessed for ever: thou hast made him exceeding glad with thy countenance. For the king *trusteth* in the LORD, and through the mercy of the most High he shall not be moved. **THINE HAND SHALL FIND OUT ALL THINE ENEMIES: THY RIGHT HAND SHALL FIND OUT THOSE THAT <u>H-A-T-E</u> THEE. Thou shalt make them as a FIERY OVEN in the time of thine ANGER: the LORD**

shall swallow them up in his WRATH, and the FIRE shall devour them. Their fruit shalt thou destroy from the earth, and their seed from among the children of men. *For* **THEY INTENDED EVIL AGAINST THEE:** they imagined a MISCHIEVOUS DEVICE, which they are not able to perform. Therefore shalt thou make them turn their back, when thou shalt make ready thine arrows upon thy strings against the face of them. *Be thou exalted, LORD, in thine own strength: so will we sing and praise thy power.* (Psalm 21:1-*13)*

Ye that fear the LORD, PRAISE HIM; all ye the seed of Jacob, *GLORIFY HIM;* and *FEAR HIM,* all ye the seed of Israel. *For HE HATH NOT <u>DESPISED</u> nor <u>ABHORRED</u> THE AFFLICTION OF THE AFFLICTED;* neither hath he hid his face from him; *but when he cried unto him,* **he heard.** (Psalm 22:23-24)

JUDGE ME, O LORD; for I have walked in mine integrity: I have trusted also in the LORD; therefore I shall not slide. EXAMINE ME, O LORD, and PROVE ME; TRY MY REINS and MY HEART. <u>For thy lovingkindness is before mine eyes: and I have walked in thy truth.</u> <u>I have not sat with vain persons, neither will I go in with dissemblers.</u> <u>I have **H-A-T-E-D** the congregation of evil doers; and will not sit with the wicked.</u> I will wash mine hands in innocency: so will I compass thine altar, O LORD: That I may publish with the voice of thanksgiving, and tell of all thy wondrous works. LORD, <u>I have loved the habitation of thy house,</u> and the place where thine honour dwelleth. Gather not my soul with sinners, nor my life with bloody men: In whose hands is MISCHIEF, and their right hand is full of BRIBES. But as for me, *I WILL WALK IN MINE INTEGRITY:* redeem me, and be merciful unto me. My foot standeth in an even place: in the congregations will I bless the LORD. (Psalm 26:1-12)

In thee, O LORD, do I put my trust; let me never be ashamed: deliver me in thy righteousness. Bow down thine ear to me; deliver me speedily: be thou my strong rock, for an house of defence to save me. For thou art my rock and my fortress; therefore for thy name's sake lead me, and guide me. **Pull me out of the net that they have laid privily for me:** for thou art my strength. Into thine hand I commit my spirit: thou hast redeemed me, O LORD God of truth. I HAVE **H-A-T-E-D** THEM THAT REGARD LYING VANITIES: *but* I trust in the LORD. (Psalm 31:1-6)

I will bless the LORD at all times: his praise shall continually be in my mouth. My soul shall make her boast in the LORD: the humble shall hear thereof, and be glad. O magnify the LORD with me, and let us exalt his name together. I sought the LORD, and he heard me, and delivered me from all my fears. They looked unto him, and were lightened: and their faces were not ashamed. *This poor man cried, and the LORD heard him, and saved him out of all his troubles.* The angel of the LORD encampeth round about them that fear him, and delivereth them. O taste and see that the LORD is good: blessed is the man that trusteth in him. O FEAR THE LORD, ye his saints: for there is no want to them that fear him. The young lions do lack, and suffer hunger: but they that seek the LORD shall not want any good thing. **Come, ye children,** hearken unto me: I will teach you the FEAR of the LORD. (Q) What man is he that desireth life, and loveth many days, that he may see good? (A) KEEP THY TONGUE FROM EVIL, and THY LIPS FROM SPEAKING GUILE. DEPART FROM EVIL, and DO GOOD; SEEK PEACE, and PURSUE IT. *The eyes of the LORD are upon the righteous, and his ears are open unto their cry.* **The face of the LORD is <u>against</u> them that do EVIL, to cut off the remembrance of them from the earth.** The righteous cry, and the LORD heareth, and delivereth them out of all their troubles. *The LORD is nigh unto them that are of a <u>broken heart</u>; and saveth such as be of a <u>contrite spirit</u>. Many are the afflictions of the righteous: but the LORD delivereth him out of them all.* He keepeth all his bones: not one of them is broken. **EVIL** SHALL SLAY THE WICKED: and THEY THAT **H-A-T-E** THE RIGHTEOUS SHALL BE DESOLATE. The LORD redeemeth the soul of his servants: and none of them that trust in him shall be desolate. (Psalm 34:1-22)

The transgression of the WICKED saith within my heart, that **there is NO FEAR OF GOD before his eyes.** *For* HE FLATTERETH HIMSELF IN HIS OWN EYES, UNTIL HIS INIQUITY BE FOUND TO BE **<u>HATEFUL</u>. The words of his mouth are INIQUITY and DECEIT: he hath left off to be wise, and to do good. He deviseth mischief upon his bed; he setteth himself in a way that is not good;**

<u>HE A-B-H-O-R-R-E-T-H</u> <u>NOT</u> <u>EVIL</u>.

Thy mercy, O LORD, is in the heavens; and thy faithfulness reacheth unto the clouds. Thy righteousness is like the great mountains; thy judgments are a great deep: O LORD, thou preservest man and beast. How excellent is thy lovingkindness, O God! **therefore** *the children of men put their trust under the shadow of thy wings. They shall be abundantly satisfied with the fatness of thy house; and thou shalt make them drink of the river of thy pleasures. For with thee is the fountain of life: in thy light shall we see light. O continue thy lovingkindness unto them that know thee; and thy righteousness to the upright in heart.* Let not the foot of pride come against me, and let not the hand of the wicked remove me. **There are THE WORKERS OF INIQUITY FALLEN: they are cast down, and shall not be able to rise.** (Psalm 36:1-12)

My heart is inditing a good matter: I speak of the things which I have made touching THE KING: my tongue is the pen of a ready writer. <u>Thou art fairer than the children of men: grace is poured into thy lips</u>: *therefore* <u>God hath blessed thee for ever</u>. Gird thy sword upon thy thigh, O most mighty, with thy glory and thy majesty. And in thy majesty ride prosperously *because of <u>truth</u> and <u>meekness</u> and <u>righteousness</u>;* and thy right hand shall teach thee terrible things. Thine arrows are sharp in the heart of the king's enemies; whereby the people fall under thee. Thy throne, O God, is for ever and ever: the sceptre of thy kingdom is a right sceptre. ***Thou lovest righteousness, and*** **<u>H-A-T-E-S-T</u> <u>WICKEDNESS</u>:** therefore God, thy God, hath anointed thee with the oil of gladness above thy fellows. (Psalm 45:1-7)

30

Have mercy upon me, O God, according to thy lovingkindness: according unto the multitude of thy tender mercies blot out my transgressions. Wash me throughly from mine iniquity, and cleanse me from my sin. *For* **I ACKNOWLEDGE MY TRANSGRESSIONS: and MY SIN IN EVER BEFORE ME. <u>AGAINST</u> <u>THEE</u>, <u>THEE</u> <u>ONLY</u>, HAVE I SINNED, and DONE THIS EVIL IN THY SIGHT:** that thou mightest be justified when thou speakest, and be clear when thou judgest. Behold, I was shapen in iniquity; and in sin did my mother conceive me. Behold, THOU DESIREST TRUTH IN THE INWARD PARTS: and in the hidden part thou shalt make me to know wisdom. Purge me with hyssop, and I shall be clean: wash me, and I shall be whiter than snow. Make me to hear joy and gladness; that the bones which thou hast broken may rejoice. HIDE THY FACE FROM MY SINS, *and* BLOT OUT ALL MINE INIQUITIES. *Create in me a <u>clean heart</u>, O God; and renew a <u>right spirit</u> within me.* Cast me not away from thy presence; and take not thy holy spirit from me. Restore unto me the joy of thy salvation; and uphold me with thy free spirit. *T-h-e-n* will I teach transgressors thy ways; and sinners shall be converted unto thee. Deliver me from bloodguiltiness, O God, thou God of my salvation: and my tongue shall sing aloud of thy righteousness. O Lord, open thou my lips; and my mouth shall shew forth thy praise. For thou desirest not sacrifice; else would I give it: thou delightest not in burnt offering. ***The sacrifices of God are a <u>broken spirit</u>: <u>a broken and a contrite heart</u>, O God, thou wilt n-o-t <u>DESPISE</u>.*** Do good in thy good pleasure unto Zion: build thou the walls of Jerusalem. Then shalt thou be pleased with the sacrifices of righteousness, with burnt offering and whole burnt offering: then shall they offer bullocks upon thine altar. (Psalm 51:1-19)

The FOOL hath said in his heart, <u>There is no God</u>. **Corrupt are they, and have done ABOMINABLE INIQUITY: there is none that doeth good.** <u>God looked down from heaven upon the children of men, to see if there were any that did understand, that did seek God.</u> **E-v-e-r-y <u>o-n-e</u> <u>o-f</u> <u>t-h-e-m</u> is GONE BACK: they are altogether become FILTHY; there is <u>n-o-n-e</u> that doeth good, <u>n-o</u>, <u>n-o-t</u> <u>o-n-e</u>.** Have the workers of iniquity *no* knowledge? who eat up my people as they eat bread: they have *not* called upon God. **THERE WERE THEY IN GREAT FEAR, WHERE NO FEAR WAS: for GOD HATH SCATTERED THE BONES OF HIM THAT ENCAMPETH AGAINST THEE: THOU HAST PUT THEM TO SHAME, *because* GOD HATH <u>D-E-S-P-I-S-E-D</u> THEM.** Oh that the salvation of Israel were come out of Zion! When God bringeth back the captivity of his people, Jacob shall rejoice, and Israel shall be glad. (Psalm 53:1-6)

For it was not an enemy that reproached me; then I could have borne it: neither was it he that **HATED** me that did magnify himself against me; then I would have hid myself from him: ***B-u-t* it was THOU, a man <u>mine equal</u>, <u>my guide</u>, and <u>mine acquaintance</u>.** (Psalm 55:12-13)

LET GOD ARISE, LET HIS ENEMIES BE SCATTERED: LET THEM ALSO THAT H-A-T-E HIM F-L-E-E BEFORE HIM. As smoke is driven away, so drive them away: as wax melteth before the fire, **so let the wicked perish at the presence of God.** *B-u-t let the* <u>*righteous*</u> *be glad; let them rejoice before God: yea, let them exceedingly rejoice. Sing unto God, sing praises to his name: extol him that rideth upon the heavens by his name* JAH, *and rejoice before him.* A father of the fatherless, and a judge of the widows, is God in his holy habitation. God setteth the solitary in families: he bringeth out those which are bound with chains: but the rebellious dwell in a dry land. O God, when thou wentest forth before thy people, when thou didst march through the wilderness; Selah: The earth shook, the heavens also dropped at the presence of God: even Sinai itself was moved at the presence of God, the God of Israel. *Thou, O God, didst send a plentiful rain, whereby thou didst confirm thine inheritance, when it was weary.* Thy congregation hath dwelt therein: thou, O God, hast prepared of thy goodness for the poor. The Lord gave the word: great was the company of those that published it. Kings of armies did flee apace: and she that tarried at home divided the spoil. <u>Though ye have lien among the pots,</u> *yet shall ye be as the wings of a dove covered with silver, and her feathers with yellow gold.* When the Almighty scattered kings in it, it was white as snow in Salmon. The hill of God is as the hill of Bashan; an high hill as the hill of Bashan. Why leap ye, ye high hills? this is the hill which God desireth to dwell in; yea, the LORD will dwell in it for ever. The chariots of God are twenty thousand, even thousands of angels: the Lord is among them, as in Sinai, in the holy place. Thou hast ascended on high, thou hast led captivity captive: thou hast received gifts for men; yea, for the rebellious also, that the LORD God might dwell among them.

Blessed be the Lord, who daily loadeth us with benefits, even the God of our salvation. Selah. (Psalm 68:1-19)

I will praise the name of God with a song, and will magnify him with thanksgiving. THIS ALSO SHALL PLEASE THE LORD better than an ox or bullock that hath horns and hoofs. The humble shall see this, and be glad: and your heart shall live that seek God. *For the LORD heareth the poor, and DESPISETH n-o-t his prisoners.* Let the heaven and earth praise him, the seas, and every thing that moveth therein. For God will save Zion, and will build the cities of Judah: that they may dwell there, and have it in possession. The seed also of his servants shall inherit it: and they that love his name shall dwell therein. (Psalm 69:30-36)

Truly God is good to Israel, even to such as are of a clean heart. *But* as for me, MY FEET WERE ALMOST GONE; MY STEPS HAD WELL NIGH SLIPPED. **For I was e-n-v-i-o-u-s at the FOOLISH, when I saw the prosperity of the WICKED.** For there are no bands in their death: *but* their strength is firm. They are *not* in trouble as other men; *neither* are they plagued like other men. ***Therefore*** PRIDE compasseth them about as a chain; VIOLENCE covereth them as a garment. Their eyes stand out with fatness: they have more than heart could wish. They are CORRUPT, and SPEAK WICKEDLY concerning oppression: they SPEAK LOFTILY. They set their mouth against the heavens, and their tongue walketh through the earth. Therefore his people return hither: and waters of a full cup are wrung out to them. And they say, HOW DOTH GOD KNOW? *and* IS

THERE KNOWLEDGE IN THE MOST HIGH? Behold, these are the ungodly, who prosper in the world; they increase in riches. **Verily I have cleansed my heart in vain, and washed my hands in innocency. For all the day long have I been plagued, and chastened every morning.** If I say, I will speak thus; behold, I should offend against the generation of thy children. When I thought to know this, it was too painful for me; *U-n-t-i-l* I went into the sanctuary of God; *t-h-e-n* **UNDERSTOOD I THEIR END.** Surely thou didst set *them* in slippery places: thou castedst *them* down into destruction. How are *they* brought into desolation, as in a moment! *they* are utterly consumed with terrors. As a dream when one awaketh; **so, O Lord, when *thou* awakest, *thou* shalt D-E-S-P-I-S-E THEIR IMAGE.** Thus my heart was grieved, and I was pricked in my reins. SO FOOLISH WAS I, and IGNORANT: I was as a beast before thee. *Nevertheless* I am continually with thee: thou hast holden me by my right hand. *Thou shalt guide me with thy counsel, and afterward receive me to glory. Whom have I in heaven but thee? and there is* **none** *upon earth that I desire beside thee.* My flesh and my heart faileth: *but* GOD IS THE STRENGTH OF MY HEART, and my portion for ever. For, lo, **they that are far from thee shall perish: thou hast destroyed all them that go a WHORING from thee.** *But* it is good for *me* to draw near to God: I have put my trust in the Lord GOD, that I may declare all thy works. (Psalm 73:1-28)

Yet they TEMPTED and PROVOKED the most high God, and KEPT NOT HIS TESTIMONIES: *But* TURNED BACK, and dealt UNFAITHFULLY like their fathers: *they* were turned aside like a deceitful bow. *For* THEY PROVOKED HIM TO ANGER with their high places, and MOVED HIM TO JEALOUSY with their graven images. **When God heard this, he was WROTH, and GREATLY A-B-H-O-R-R-E-D his heritage:** (Psalm 78:56-59)

*Sing aloud unto God our strength: make a joyful noise unto the God of Jacob. Take a psalm, and bring hither the timbrel, the pleasant harp with the psaltery. **Blow up the trumpet in the new moon, in the time appointed, on our solemn feast day.** For this was a statute for Israel, and a law of the God of Jacob.* This he ordained in Joseph for a testimony, when he went out through the land of Egypt: where I heard a language that I understood not. I removed his shoulder from the burden: his hands were delivered from the pots. Thou calledst in trouble, and I delivered thee; I answered thee in the secret place of thunder: I *proved* thee at the waters of Meribah. Selah. Hear, O my people, and I will testify unto thee: O Israel, *if* thou wilt hearken unto me; There shall no strange god be in thee; *neither* shalt thou worship any strange god. I am the LORD thy God, which brought thee out of the land of Egypt: open thy mouth wide, and I will fill it. *B-u-t* my people would *not* hearken to my voice; and Israel would none of me. *So* **I GAVE THEM UP UNTO THEIR OWN HEART'S LUST: and THEY WALKED (LIVED) IN THEIR OWN COUNSELS. Oh that my people had hearkened unto me, and Israel had walked in *my* ways!** I should *soon* have subdued their enemies, and turned my hand against their adversaries. **THE H-A-T-E-R-S OF THE LORD**

SHOULD HAVE SUBMITTED THEMSELVES UNTO HIM: but their time should have endured for ever. He should have fed them also with the finest of the wheat: and with honey out of the rock should I have satisfied thee. (Psalm 81:1-16)

Keep *not* thou silence, O God: hold *not* thy peace, and be *not* still, O God. **For, lo, thine enemies make a tumult: and THEY THAT H-A-T-E THEE HAVE LIFTED UP THE HEAD.** They have taken CRAFTY COUNSEL against thy people, and consulted against thy hidden ones. They have said, Come, and let us cut them off from being a nation; that the name of Israel may be no more in remembrance. For they have consulted together with one consent: they are confederate against thee: (Psalm 83:1-5)

For THE LORD IS OUR DEFENCE; and the Holy One of Israel is our king. Then thou spakest in vision to thy holy one, and saidst, I have laid help upon one that is mighty; I have exalted one chosen out of the people. I have found David my servant; with my holy oil have I anointed him: With whom my hand shall be established: mine arm also shall strengthen him. The enemy shall not exact upon him; nor the son of wickedness afflict him. **And I will beat down his foes before his face, and plague them that H-A-T-E him.** *But* my faithfulness and my mercy shall be with him: and in my name shall his horn be exalted. I will set his hand also in the sea, and his right hand in the rivers. He shall cry unto me, THOU ART MY FATHER, MY GOD, and THE ROCK OF MY SALVATION. (Psalm 89:18-26)

But thou hast CAST OFF and <u>A-B-H-O-R-R-E-D</u>, thou hast been wroth with <u>thine anointed</u>. Thou hast made <u>VOID THE COVENANT</u> of thy servant: thou hast profaned <u>his crown</u> by casting it to the ground. Thou hast broken down all his hedges; thou hast brought his strong holds to ruin. All that pass by the way spoil him: he is a reproach to his neighbours. Thou hast set up the right hand of his adversaries; thou hast made all his enemies to rejoice. Thou hast also turned the edge of his sword, and hast not made him to stand in the battle. Thou hast made his glory to cease, and cast <u>his throne</u> down to the ground. The days of his youth hast thou shortened: thou hast covered him with shame. Selah. HOW LONG, LORD? WILT THOU HIDE THYSELF FOR EVER? SHALL THY WRATH BURN LIKE FIRE? (Psalm 89:38-46)

The LORD reigneth; let the earth rejoice; let the multitude of isles be glad thereof. **Clouds and darkness are round about him: righteousness and judgment are the habitation of his throne.** A **fire goeth before him, and burneth up his enemies round about.** *His lightnings enlightened the world: the earth saw, and trembled. The hills melted like wax at the presence of the LORD, at the presence of the Lord of the whole earth. The heavens declare his righteousness, and all the people see his glory.* **Confounded be all they that serve graven images, that boast themselves of idols: worship him, all ye gods.** *Zion heard, and was glad; and the daughters of Judah rejoiced because of thy judgments, O LORD. For thou, LORD, art high above all the earth: thou art exalted far above all gods.* **YE THAT LOVE THE**

LORD, H-A-T-E EVIL: *he preserveth the souls of his saints; he delivereth them out of the hand of the wicked. Light is sown for the righteous, and gladness for the upright in heart. Rejoice in the LORD, ye righteous; and give thanks at the remembrance of his holiness.* (Psalm 97:1-12)

I will sing of mercy and judgment: unto thee, O LORD, will I sing.

I WILL

B-E-H-A-V-E M-Y-S-E-L-F

WISELY IN A PERFECT WAY.

O when wilt thou come unto me? I will walk within my house with a perfect heart. **I will set *no* WICKED thing before mine eyes: I H-A-T-E the work of them that TURN ASIDE; it shall not cleave to me. A FROWARD HEART shall depart from me: I will not know a WICKED PERSON. Whoso privily SLANDERETH HIS NEIGHBOUR, him will I cut off: him that hath an HIGH LOOK and a PROUD HEART will not I suffer.** Mine eyes shall be upon the faithful of the land, that they may dwell with me: he that WALKETH IN A PERFECT WAY, he shall serve me. **He that worketh DECEIT shall not dwell within my house: he that TELLETH LIES shall not tarry in my sight. I will early destroy all the WICKED of the land; that I may cut off all WICKED DOERS from the city of the LORD.** (Psalm 101:1-8)

When the LORD shall BUILD UP ZION, he shall appear in his glory. *He will regard the prayer of the destitute, and n-o-t DESPISE their prayer.* This shall be written for the generation to come: *and the people which shall be created shall praise the LORD.* For he hath looked down from the height of his sanctuary; from heaven did the LORD behold the earth; To hear the groaning of the prisoner; to loose those that are appointed to death; To declare the name of the LORD in Zion, and his praise in Jerusalem; When the people are gathered together, and the kingdoms, to serve the LORD. (Psalm 102:16-22)

Thus were they *defiled* WITH THEIR OWN WORKS, and went a WHORING with their own inventions. *Therefore* was the WRATH of the LORD kindled against his people, insomuch that he A-B-H-O-R-R-E-D his own inheritance. (Psalm 106:30-40)

I have not departed from thy judgments: for thou hast taught me. How sweet are thy words unto my taste! yea, sweeter than honey to my mouth! *Through thy precepts I get understanding: therefore* I H-A-T-E EVERY FALSE WAY. *THY WORD IS A LAMP UNTO MY FEET, and A LIGHT UNTO MY PATH.* I have sworn, and I will perform it, that I will keep thy righteous judgments. (Psalm 119:102-106)

Deal with thy servant according unto thy *mercy,* and teach me thy statutes. I am thy servant; give me understanding, that I may know thy testimonies. **IT IS TIME FOR THEE, LORD, TO WORK: for they have made void thy law.** *Therefore* I LOVE

THY COMMANDMENTS above gold; yea, above fine gold. Therefore I esteem all thy precepts concerning all things to be right; *and* **I H-A-T-E EVERY FALSE WAY.** Thy testimonies are wonderful: therefore doth my soul keep them. (Psalm 119:124-129)

***THY WORD** is true from the beginning: and every one of THY RIGHTEOUS JUDGMENTS endureth for ever.* Princes have persecuted me without a cause: *but **my heart** standeth in awe of THY WORD.* I rejoice at *THY WORD, as one that findeth great spoil.* **I H-A-T-E** *and* **A-B-H-O-R** LYING: *b-u-t **THY LAW** do I love.* SEVEN TIMES A DAY do I praise thee because of *THY RIGHTEOUS JUDGMENTS.* Great peace have they which love *THY LAW*: and nothing shall offend them. LORD, I have hoped for *THY SALVATION*, and done *THY COMMANDMENTS.* **My soul** hath kept *THY TESTIMONIES;* and I love them exceedingly. I have kept *THY PRECEPTS* and *THY TESTIMONIES:* for all my way are before thee. Let **my cry** come near before thee, O LORD: give me understanding according to *THY WORD.* Let **my supplication** come before thee: deliver me according to *THY WORD.* My lips shall utter praise, when thou hast taught me *THY STATUTES.* **My tongue** shall speak of *THY WORD*: for all *THY COMMANDMENTS* are righteousness. Let *THINE HAND* help me; for I have chosen *THY PRECEPTS.* I have longed for *THY SALVATION*, O LORD; and *THY LAW* is my delight. Let **my soul** live, and it shall praise thee; and let *THY JUDGMENTS* help me. **I have gone astray like a lost sheep;** seek *thy servant;* for I do not forget *THY COMMANDMENTS.* (Psalm 119:160-176)

How precious also are *thy thoughts* unto me, O God! how great is the sum of them! If I should count them, they are more in number than the sand: when I awake, I am still with thee. SURELY THOU WILT SLAY THE WICKED, OH GOD: DEPART FROM ME THEREFORE, YE BLOODY MEN. FOR THEY SPEAK AGAINST THEE WICKEDLY, and **THINE ENEMIES TAKE THY NAME IN VAIN. DO NOT I H-A-T-E THEM, O LORD, THAT H-A-T-E THEE? and AM I NOT GRIEVED WITH THOSE THAT RISE UP AGAINST THEE? I H-A-T-E THEM WITH A P-E-R-F-E-C-T H-A-T-R-E-D:** I COUNT THEM MINE ENEMIES. *S-e-a-r-c-h me,* O God, and know my heart: *t-r-y me,* and know my thoughts: And see if there be *any* wicked way in me, and *l-e-a-d me* in the way everlasting. (Psalm 139:17-24)

THE PROVERBS OF SOLOMON the son of David, king of Israel; To know <u>wisdom</u> and <u>instruction</u>; to perceive the words of <u>understanding</u>; To receive the instruction of <u>wisdom</u>, <u>justice</u>, and <u>judgment</u>, and <u>equity</u>; To give subtilty to the simple, to the young man knowledge and discretion. *A wise man will hear, and will **increase** learning; and a man of understanding shall attain unto wise counsels:* To understand a proverb, and the interpretation; the words of the wise, and their dark sayings. ***The FEAR OF THE LORD is the beginning of knowledge: b-u-t* FOOLS D-E-S-P-I-S-E WISDOM and INSTRUCTION.** (Proverbs 1:1-7)

WISDOM *crieth* without; she uttereth her voice in the streets: She *crieth* in the chief place of concourse, in the openings of the gates: in the city she uttereth her words, saying, **H-O-W L-O-N-G, YE SIMPLE ONES, WILL YE LOVE SIMPLICITY?** *and* **THE SCORNERS DELIGHT IN THEIR SCORNING,** *and* **FOOLS <u>H-A-T-E</u> KNOWLEDGE?** TURN YOU AT MY REPROOF: *behold, I will pour out <u>my spirit</u> unto you, I will make known my words unto you. **Because I have called, and <u>ye refused</u>; I have stretched out my hand, and <u>no man regarded</u>;** But ye have set at nought all my counsel, and would none of my reproof: I ALSO WILL **<u>LAUGH</u>** AT YOUR CALAMITY; I WILL **<u>MOCK</u>** WHEN YOUR FEAR COMETH; When your fear cometh as desolation, and your destruction cometh as a whirlwind; when distress and anguish cometh upon you. **T-h-e-n shall they call upon me, b-u-t I will not answer; (t-h-e-n) they shall seek me early, b-u-t they shall not find me:** *F-o-r* **that THEY <u>H-A-T-E-D</u> KNOWLEDGE, and DID NOT CHOOSE THE FEAR OF THE LORD: THEY WOULD NONE OF MY COUNSEL: THEY <u>D-I-S-P-I-S-E-D</u> ALL MY REPROOF.** *Therefore* **shall they eat of the fruit of THEIR OWN WAY, and be filled with THEIR OWN DEVICES. For the turning away of the simple shall slay them, and the prosperity of fools shall destroy them.** *B-u-t* *whoso hearkeneth unto me shall dwell safely, and shall be quiet from fear of evil.* (Proverbs 1:20-33)

43

MY SON, attend unto my wisdom, and bow thine ear to my understanding: That thou mayest regard discretion, and that thy lips may keep knowledge. For the lips of **a strange woman** drop as an honeycomb, and her mouth is smoother than oil: But her end is bitter as wormwood, sharp as a two-edged sword. Her feet go down to DEATH; her steps take hold on HELL. Lest thou shouldest ponder the path of life, her ways are moveable, that thou canst not know them. Hear me now therefore, O ye children, and depart *not* from the words of my mouth. **Remove thy way FAR from her,** and come not nigh the door of her house: Lest thou give thine honour unto others, and thy years unto the cruel: Lest strangers be filled with thy wealth; and thy labours be in the house of a stranger; And thou mourn at the last, when thy flesh and thy body are consumed, And say, **HOW HAVE I H-A-T-E-D INSTRUCTION, *and* MY HEART D-E-S-P-I-S-E-D REPROOF; *and* HAVE NOT OBEYED THE VOICE OF MY TEACHERS,** *nor* **INCLINED MINE EAR TO THEM THAT INSTRUCTED ME!** (Proverbs 5:1-13)

These SIX things doth the LORD H-A-T-E: yea, SEVEN are an A-B-O-M-I-N-A-T-I-O-N unto him: (1) A proud look, (2) a lying tongue, and (3) hands that shed innocent blood, (4) An heart that deviseth wicked imaginations, (5) feet that be swift in running to mischief, (6) A false witness that speaketh lies, *and* (7) he that soweth discord among brethren. **My son, keep thy father's commandment, and forsake not the law of thy mother:** Bind them continually upon thine heart, and tie them about thy neck. When thou GOEST, it shall lead thee; when thou SLEEPEST, it shall keep thee; and when thou AWAKEST, it shall talk with thee. For the commandment is a lamp; and the law is light; and REPROOFS OF INSTRUCTION ARE THE WAY OF LIFE: (Proverbs 6:16-23)

For WISDOM is better than *rubies;* and all the things that may be desired are *not* to be compared to it. I wisdom dwell with prudence, and find out knowledge of witty inventions. **THE FEAR OF THE LORD IS TO H-A-T-E EVIL: PRIDE, *and* ARROGANCY, *and* THE EVIL WAY, *and* THE FROWARD MOUTH, DO I H-A-T-E.** Counsel is mine, and sound wisdom: I am understanding; I have strength. (Proverbs 8:11-14)

Hear instruction, and BE WISE, and refuse it not. *Blessed is the man that heareth me,* watching daily at my gates, waiting at the posts of my doors. For whoso findeth me findeth LIFE, and shall obtain FAVOUR of the LORD. ***B-u-t* HE THAT SINNETH AGAINST ME WRONGETH HIS *OWN* SOUL: ALL THEY THAT H-A-T-E ME LOVE DEATH.** (Proverbs 8:33-36)

Reprove not a scorner, lest he H-A-T-E thee: *rebuke a wise man, and he will l-o-v-e thee.* (Proverbs 9:8)

He that is VOID OF WISDOM **D-E-S-P-I-S-E-T-H** his neighbour: *but a man of understanding holdeth his peace.* (Proverbs 11:12)

Whoso loveth instruction loveth knowledge: **but he that H-A-T-E-T-H reproof is BRUTISH.** (Proverbs 12:1)

The wicked are OVERTHROWN and are <u>not</u>: *b-u-t the house of the righteous shall stand. A man shall be commended according to his wisdom: but* **he that is of a PERVERSE HEART shall be <u>D-E-S-P-I-S-E-D</u>. HE THAT IS <u>D-E-S-P-I-S-E-D</u>, and hath a servant, is better than he that honoureth himself, and lacketh bread.** *A righteous man regardeth the life of his beast: but* **the tender mercies of the wicked are CRUEL.** (Proverbs 12:7-10)

A righteous man **<u>HATETH</u> LYING:** *but* **a WICKED man is LOATHSOME, and <u>cometh to shame</u>.** *Righteousness keepeth him that is upright in the way: but* **wickedness OVERTHROWETH the sinner.** (Proverbs 13:5-6)

WHOSO <u>D-E-S-P-I-S-E-T-H</u> THE WORD SHALL BE <u>DESTROYED</u>: *b-u-t he that feareth the COMMANDMENT shall be rewarded.* **THE LAW OF THE WISE IS A FOUNTAIN OF LIFE, TO DEPART FROM THE SNARES OF DEATH.** *Good understanding giveth favour: but* **the way of transgressors is HARD.** (Proverbs 13:13-15)

He that spareth his rod <u>H-A-T-E-T-H</u> his son: *but he that loveth him <u>c-h-a-s-t-e-n-e-t-h</u> him betimes.* (Proverbs 13:24)

He that is <u>soon angry</u> dealeth FOOLISHLY: *and* **a man of <u>wicked devices</u> is <u>H-A-T-E-D</u>.** (Proverbs 14:17)

He that <u>DESPISETH</u> HIS NEIGHBOUR SINNETH: *but he that hath MERCY on the poor, HAPPY is he.* (Proverbs 14:21)

A FOOL D-E-S-P-I-S-E-T-H his father's instruction: *but* *he* *that* *regardeth* *reproof* *is* *prudent.* (Proverbs 15:5)

The way of the WICKED is an a-b-o-m-i-n-a-t-i-o-n unto the LORD: *b-u-t* *he* *loveth* *him* *that* *followeth* *after* *RIGHTEOUSNESS.* Correction is grievous unto him that forsaketh the way: and HE THAT H-A-T-E-T-H REPROOF SHALL DIE. HELL and DESTRUCTION are before the LORD: how much more then the hearts of the children of men? A SCORNER loveth not one that reproveth him: neither will he go unto the wise. (Proverbs 15:9-12)

A *wise* *son* *maketh* *a* *glad* *father:* *but* a foolish man DESPISETH his mother. Folly is joy to him that is DESTITUTE of wisdom: *but* *a* *man* *of* *understanding* *walketh* *uprightly.* Without counsel purposes are disappointed: *but* *in* *the* *multitude* *of* *counsellors* *they* *are* *established.* *A* *man* *hath* *joy* *by* *the* *answer* *of* *his* *mouth:* *and* *a* *word* *spoken* *in* *due* *season,* *how* *good* *is* *it!* *The* *way* *of* *life* *is* *above* *to* *the* *wise,* THAT HE MAY DEPART FROM HELL BENEATH. The LORD will DESTROY the house of the PROUD: *but* *he* *will* *establish* *the* *border* *of* *the* *widow.* The thoughts of the WICKED are an a-b-o-m-i-n-a-t-i-o-n to the LORD: *but* *the* *words* *of* *the* *pure* *are* *pleasant* *words.* He that is greedy of gain troubleth his own house; *but* *HE* *THAT* *H-A-T-E-T-H* *GIFTS* *SHALL* *LIVE.* *The* *heart* *of* *the* *righteous* *studieth* *to* *answer:* *but* the mouth of the WICKED poureth out evil things. The LORD is far from the wicked: *but* *he* *heareth* *the* *prayer* *of* *the* *righteous.* *The* *light* *of* *the* *eyes* *rejoiceth* *the* *heart:*

and a good report maketh the bones fat. The ear that heareth the reproof of life abideth among the wise. **He that refuseth instruction D-E-S-P-I-S-E-T-H his own soul:** *but he that heareth reproof getteth understanding. The FEAR OF THE LORD is the instruction of wisdom; and before honour is humility.* (Proverbs 15:20-33)

He that <u>keepeth the commandment</u> keepeth his own soul; ***but* he that DESPISETH his ways shall die.** (Proverb 19:16)

The mouth of strange women is a deep pit: he that is A-B-H-O-R-R-E-D OF THE LORD shall fall therein. (Proverbs 22:14)

Speak not in the ears of a FOOL: *for* **HE WILL <u>D-E-S-P-I-S-E</u> THE WISDOM OF THY WORDS.** (Proverbs 23:9)

Hearken unto thy <u>father</u> that begat thee, and **DESPISE NOT** *thy <u>mother</u> when she is old. Buy the truth, and sell it not; also wisdom, and instruction, and understanding.* (Proverbs 23:22-23)

He that saith unto the **WICKED, Thou are righteous; him shall the people CURSE, nations shall <u>A-B-H-O-R</u> him:** (Proverbs 24:24)

As a MAD MAN who casteth firebrands, arrows, and death, So is the man that DECEIVETH his neighbour, and saith, **Am not I in sport?** Where no wood is, there the fire goeth out: so where there is no TALEBEEARER the strife ceaseth. As coals are to burning coals, and wood to fire; so is a

CONTENTIOUS man to kindle strife. The words of a TALEBEARER are as wounds, and they go down into the innermost parts of the belly. BURNING LIPS and a WICKED HEART are like a potsherd covered with silver dross. **He that H-A-T-E-T-H dissembleth with his lips, and layeth up DECEIT within him;** When he speaketh fair, <u>believe him not</u>: for there are SEVEN ABOMINATIONS in his heart. **Whose <u>H-A-T-R-E-D</u> is covered by DECEIT,** his wickedness shall be shewed before the whole congregation. **WHOSO DIGGETH A PIT SHALL FALL THEREIN: and HE THAT ROLLETH A STONE, IT WILL RETURN UPON HIM. A LYING TONGUE <u>H-A-T-E-T-H</u> those that are afflicted by it; and a flattering mouth worketh ruin.** (Proverbs 26:18-28)

The prince that wanteth understanding is also a great oppressor: *but he that **<u>HATETH COVETOUSNESS</u>** shall prolong his days.* (Proverbs 28:16)

If **a wise man <u>contendeth</u> with a FOOLISH man, whether he rage or laugh, THERE IS NO REST. The bloodthirsty <u>H-A-T-E</u> the upright:** *but the just seek his soul.* **A FOOL uttereth all his mind:** *but a WISE man keepeth it in till afterwards.* (Proverbs 29:9-11)

An ANGRY MAN stirreth up strife, and a FURIOUS man aboundeth in transgression. A man's PRIDE shall bring him low: *but honour shall uphold the humble in spirit.* **WHOSO IS PARTNER WITH A THIEF <u>H-A-T-E-T-H</u> HIS OWN SOUL: he heareth CURSING, and**

bewrayeth it not. The FEAR OF <u>MAN</u> **bringeth a snare:** *but whoso putteth his trust in the* L*ORD* *shall be safe.* **Many seek the <u>ruler's</u> favour;** *but every man's judgment cometh from the* L*ORD.* **AN <u>UNJUST</u> MAN IS AN A-B-O-M-I-N-A-T-I-O-N TO THE JUST:** *and* HE THAT IS UPRIGHT IN THE WAY IS A-B-O-M-I-N-A-T-I-O-N TO THE <u>WICKED</u>. (Proverbs 29:22-27)

The eye that MOCKETH at his father, and <u>D-E-S-P-I-S-E-T-H</u> TO OBEY his mother, the ravens of the valley shall pick it out, and the young eagles shall eat it. (Proverbs 30:17)

WOE unto them that <u>call evil good, and good evil</u>; that put <u>darkness for light, and light for darkness</u>; that put <u>bitter for sweet, and sweet for bitter</u>! WOE unto them that are WISE IN THEIR OWN EYES, and PRUDENT IN THEIR OWN SIGHT! WOE unto them that are <u>mighty to drink wine</u>, and men of strength to <u>mingle strong drink</u>: Which justify the wicked for reward, and take away the righteousness of the righteous from him! *Therefore* **as the fire devoureth the STUBBLE, and the flame consumeth the CHAFF, so their root shall be as ROTTENNESS, and their blossom shall go up as DUST:** *because* **THEY HAVE CAST AWAY THE LAW OF THE LORD OF HOSTS,** *and* **<u>D-E-S-P-I-S-E-D</u> THE WORD OF THE HOLY ONE OF ISRAEL.** (Isaiah 5:20-24)

Wherefore thus saith the Holy One of Israel, *Because* YE <u>D-E-S-P-I-S-E</u> THIS WORD, **and trust in oppression and perverseness, and stay thereon:** *Therefore* this iniquity shall be to you as a BREACH READY TO FALL, swelling out in a high wall, whose BREAKING COMETH SUDDENLY at an instant. **And he shall break it as the breaking of the potters' vessel that is broken in pieces; he shall *not* spare:** so that there shall not be found in the bursting of it a sherd to take fire from the hearth, or to take water withal out of the pit. For thus saith the Lord GOD, the Holy One of Israel; *In returning and rest shall ye be saved; in quietness and in confidence shall be your strength:* **and YE WOULD <u>NOT</u>.** (Isaiah 30:12-15)

He that WALKETH righteously, and SPEAKETH uprightly; *he that DESPISETH the gain of oppressions,* that SHAKETH HIS HANDS *from* holding of bribes, that STOPPETH HIS EARS *from* hearing of blood, and SHUTTETH HIS EYES *from* seeing evil; *He shall dwell on high:* his place of defence shall be the munitions of rocks: bread shall be given him; his waters shall be sure. *Thine eyes shall see the king in his beauty:* they shall behold the land that is very far off. (Isaiah 33:15-17)

(Q) Who hath believed our report? and to whom is the arm of the LORD revealed? (A) <u>For he shall grow up before him as a tender plant, and as a root out of a dry ground: he hath NO FORM NOR COMELINESS; and when we shall see him, there is NO BEAUTY that we should desire him. -He is DESPISED and REJECTED OF MEN; A MAN OF SORROWS, and ACQUAINTED WITH GRIEF: and we hid as it were our faces from him; HE WAS DESPISED and WE ESTEEMED HIM NOT.</u> ***Surely he hath borne our griefs, and carried our sorrows:*** <u>yet we did esteem him stricken, smitten of</u>

51

God, and afflicted. -*But* he was wounded for our transgressions, he was bruised for our iniquities: the chastisement of our peace was upon him; and with his stripes we are healed. -All we like sheep have gone astray; we have turned every one to his own way; and the LORD hath laid on HIM the iniquity of US all. -He was oppressed, and he was afflicted, yet he opened not his mouth: he is brought as a lamb to the slaughter, and as a sheep before her shearers is dumb, so he openeth not his mouth. -He was taken from prison and from judgment: and who shall declare his generation? for he was cut off out of the land of the living: for the transgression of my people was he stricken. -And he made his grave with the wicked, and with the rich in his death; *because he had done no violence, neither was any DECEIT in his mouth.* **Yet it pleased the LORD to BRUISE HIM; he hath put him to grief: when thou shalt make *his* soul AN OFFERING FOR SIN, he shall see his seed, he shall prolong his days, and the pleasure of the LORD shall prosper in his hand. He shall see of the travail of his soul, and shall be satisfied: by his knowledge shall my righteous servant justify many; for HE SHALL BEAR THEIR INIQUITIES.** *Therefore* will I divide him a portion with the GREAT, and he shall divide the spoil with the STRONG; *because* he hath poured out his soul unto death: and **he was numbered with the transgressors;** *and he bare the sin of many, and made INTERCESSION FOR THE TRANSGRESSORS.* (Isaiah 53:1-12)

Hear the word of the Lord, YE THAT <u>TREMBLE</u> AT HIS WORD; **Your brethren that <u>HATED</u> you, that cast you out for my name's sake,** said,

52

Let the Lord be glorified: but he shall appear to your joy, and **they shall be ashamed.** (Isaiah 66: 5)

I have <u>forsaken</u> **MINE house,** *I* **have** <u>left</u> **MINE heritage;** *I* **have** <u>given</u> **the dearly beloved of MY soul into the hand of her enemies. MINE heritage is unto** *ME* **as a lion in the forest;** <u>it crieth</u> <u>out</u> *against* <u>ME</u>*: therefore* **have I** <u>H-A-T-E-D</u> **it.** (Jeremiah 12:7-8)

Then said I, Ah, Lord GOD! behold, **the (false) prophets** say unto them, <u>Ye shall not see the sword, neither shall ye have famine; but I will give you assured peace in this place.</u> Then the LORD said unto me, **THE PROPHETS PROPHESY** <u>LIES</u> **IN MY NAME: I SENT THEM** <u>NOT</u>, *neither* **HAVE I COMMANDED THEM,** *neither* **SPAKE UNTO THEM: THEY PROPHESY UNTO YOU A** <u>FALSE</u> **VISION** *and* **DIVINATION, *and* A THING OF NOUGHT, *and* THE** <u>DECEIT</u> **OF THEIR HEART.** *Therefore* thus saith the LORD concerning the prophets that prophesy in my name, and I sent them *not, yet* they say, <u>Sword and famine shall not be in this land; By sword and famine shall those prophets be consumed</u>. **And the people to whom they prophesy shall be CAST OUT in the streets of Jerusalem because of the FAMINE and the SWORD; and they shall have none to bury them, them, their wives, nor their sons, nor their daughters: for I will pour** *their* **wickedness upon** *them.* Therefore thou shalt say *this* word unto them; <u>Let mine eyes run down with tears night and day, and let them not cease:</u> **for the virgin daughter of my people is broken with a GREAT BREACH, with a VERY GRIEVOUS BLOW.**

-If I go forth into the field, then behold the SLAIN WITH THE SWORD! and if I enter into the city, then behold them that are sick with FAMINE! yea, both the prophet and the priest go about into a land that they know not. -Hast thou utterly REJECTED Judah? hath thy soul **LOTHED** Zion? why hast thou SMITTEN us, and there is NO HEALING for us? we looked for peace, and there is NO GOOD; and for the time of healing, and behold TROUBLE! **We acknowledge, O LORD, our wickedness, and the iniquity of our fathers: for WE HAVE SINNED AGAINST THEE. DO NOT A-B-H-O-R US, for thy name's sake, do not disgrace the throne of thy glory: remember, break not thy covenant with us.** Are there any among the vanities of the Gentiles that can cause rain? or can the heavens give showers? art not thou he, O LORD our God? *therefore we will WAIT upon thee: for thou hast made all these things.* (Jeremiah 14:13-22)

We acknowledge, O LORD, our WICKEDNESS, and the INIQUITY of our fathers: for we have SINNED AGAINST THEE. DO NOT A-B-H-O-R US, *for thy name's sake,* **do not disgrace the throne of thy glory: remember, break not thy covenant with us.** (Jeremiah 14:20-21)

FOR MINE EYES ARE UPON A-L-L THEIR WAYS: THEY ARE N-O-T HID FROM MY FACE, *neither* **IS THEIR INIQUITY HID FROM MINE EYES.** *And* **F-I-R-S-T WILL I RECOMPENSE THEIR INIQUITY AND THEIR SIN D-O-U-B-L-E;** *b-e-c-a-u-s-e* **they have defiled my land, they have filled mine inheritance with the carcases of their detestable**

and abominable things. O Lord, my strength, and my fortress, and my refuge in the day of affliction, the Gentiles shall come unto thee from the ends of the earth, and shall say, Surely our fathers have inherited lies, vanity, and things wherein there is no profit. **Shall a man make gods unto himself, and they are no gods?** Therefore, behold, **I WILL THIS ONCE CAUSE THEM TO KNOW, I WILL CAUSE THEM TO KNOW MINE HAND *and* MY MIGHT; *and* THEY SHALL KNOW THAT MY NAME IS THE LORD.** (Jeremiah 16:17-21)

Thus saith the Lord of hosts, **Hearken *not* unto the words of the (FALSE) PROPHETS that prophesy unto you: they make you VAIN: they speak a vision of their *own* heart, and *not* out of the mouth of the Lord. They say still unto THEM THAT D-E-S-P-I-S-E ME, The Lord hath said, Ye shall have peace; and they say unto every one that WALKETH AFTER THE IMAGINATION OF HIS OWN HEART, No evil shall come upon you. For who hath stood in the counsel of the Lord, and hath perceived and heard his word? who hath marked his word, and heard it? Behold, a WHIRLWIND OF THE LORD is gone forth in FURY, even a GRIEVOUS WHIRLWIND: it shall fall grievously upon the head of the WICKED. The ANGER of the Lord shall not return, until he have executed, and till he have performed the thoughts of his heart: in the latter days ye shall consider it perfectly. I have *not* sent these prophets, *yet* they ran: I have *not* spoken to them, *yet* they prophesied.** *But* if they *had* stood in my counsel, and had caused my people to hear my words, *t-h-e-n* <u>THEY SHOULD HAVE TURNED THEM FROM THEIR EVIL WAY, and FROM THE EVIL OF THEIR DOINGS</u>. Am I a God at hand, saith the LORD, and *not a God afar off? Can any hide himself in secret places that I shall not see him?* saith the LORD. Do not I fill heaven and earth? saith the LORD. **I have heard what the prophets said, that PROPHESY LIES IN MY NAME, saying, <u>I have dreamed</u>, <u>I have dreamed</u>. How long shall this be in the heart of the prophets that prophesy LIES? yea, they are prophets of the <u>D-E-C-E-I-T</u> OF THEIR OWN HEART;** Which think to <u>cause my people to forget my name by their DREAMS</u> which they tell every man to his neighbour, as **THEIR FATHERS HAVE FORGOTTEN MY NAME FOR BAAL.** The prophet that **<u>hath a dream</u>**, let him tell a dream; and he that hath my word, *let him speak my word faithfully.* What is the CHAFF to the wheat? saith the LORD. Is not my word like as a FIRE? saith the LORD; and like a HAMMER that breaketh the rock in pieces? Therefore, behold, **I am** *against* **the prophets, saith the LORD,** that steal my words every one from his neighbour. **Behold, I am** *against* **the prophets, saith the LORD,** that use their tongues, and say, He saith. **<u>Behold, I am</u> <u>*against* them that prophesy false dreams</u>**, saith the LORD, and do tell them, and CAUSE MY PEOPLE TO ERR BY THEIR **LIES,** and BY THEIR **LIGHTNESS;** yet I sent them *not, nor* commanded them: *therefore* **they shall not profit this people AT ALL,** saith the LORD. (Jeremiah 23:16-32)

The word that came to Jeremiah concerning all the Jews which dwell in the land of Egypt, which dwell at Migdol, and at Tahpanhes, and at Noph, and in the country of Pathros, saying,   Thus saith the LORD of hosts, the God of Israel; Ye have seen all the evil that I have brought upon Jerusalem, and upon all the cities of Judah; and, behold, this day they are a DESOLATION, and no man dwelleth therein,   Because of their wickedness which they have committed **TO PROVOKE ME TO ANGER,** in that they went to burn incense, and to **SERVE OTHER GODS,** whom they knew not, neither they, ye, nor your fathers.   Howbeit I sent unto you all my servants the prophets, rising early and sending them, saying, **Oh, do** *not* **this ABOMINABLE thing that I <u>H-A-T-E</u>.** *But* **they** <u>**hearkened** *not, nor* **inclined their ear to turn from their wickedness,**</u> to burn no incense unto other gods.   **Wherefore my FURY and mine ANGER was poured forth,** and was kindled in the cities of Judah and in the streets of Jerusalem; and **they are wasted and desolate, as at this day.** (Jeremiah 44:1-6)

How hath the LORD covered the daughter of Zion with a cloud IN HIS ANGER, and cast down from heaven unto the earth the beauty of Israel, and remembered not his footstool in THE DAY OF HIS ANGER!   The LORD hath swallowed up all the habitations of Jacob, and HATH NOT PITIED: he hath thrown down in HIS WRATH the strong holds of the daughter of Judah; he hath brought them down to the ground: he hath POLLUTED the kingdom and the princes thereof.   He hath CUT OFF IN HIS FIERCE ANGER all the horn of Israel: he hath drawn back his right hand from before the enemy, and he BURNED against Jacob like a

flaming fire, which devoureth round about. He hath bent his bow LIKE AN ENEMY: he stood with his right hand AS AN ADVERSARY, and SLEW all that were pleasant to the eye in the tabernacle of the daughter of Zion: HE POURED OUT HIS FURY LIKE FIRE. The LORD was AS AN ENEMY: he hath SWALLOWED up Israel, he hath SWALLOWED up all her palaces: he hath DESTROYED his strong holds, and hath increased in the daughter of Judah MOURNING and LAMENTATION. And he hath VIOLENTLY TAKEN AWAY HIS TABERNACLE, as if it were of a garden: he hath DESTROYED his places of the assembly: the LORD hath caused the solemn feasts and sabbaths to be FORGOTTEN in Zion, and hath D-E-S-P-I-S-E-D in the INDIGNATION OF HIS ANGER the king and the priest. The LORD hath CAST OFF HIS ALTAR, HE HATH A-B-H-O-R-R-E-D HIS SANCTUARY, he hath GIVEN UP INTO THE HAND OF THE ENEMY the walls of her palaces; they have made a noise in the house of the LORD, as in the day of a solemn feast. The LORD hath PURPOSED TO DESTROY the wall of the daughter of Zion: he hath stretched out a line, HE HATH NOT WITHDRAWN HIS HAND FROM DESTROYING: therefore he made the rampart and the wall to LAMENT; they LANGUISHED together. (Lamentation 2:1-8)

Therefore thus saith the Lord GOD; BEHOLD, I, EVEN I, AM A-G-A-I-N-S-T THEE, and will execute judgments in the midst of thee in the sight of the nations. And I will do in thee that which I have *not* done, and whereunto I will *not* do any more the like, *because* OF ALL THINE ABOMINATIONS. **Therefore the fathers shall** *eat* **the sons in the midst of thee, and the sons shall** *eat* **their fathers; and I WILL EXECUTE JUDGMENTS IN THEE, and the whole remnant of thee will I SCATTER into all the winds.** Wherefore, as I live, saith the Lord GOD; Surely, *because* **thou hast DEFILED MY SANCTUARY with all thy DETESTABLE things, and with all thine ABOMINATIONS,** *therefore* **WILL I ALSO DIMINISH THEE;** *neither* **SHALL MINE EYE SPARE,** *neither* **WILL I HAVE ANY PITY.** A third part (1/3) of thee shall die with the PESTILENCE, *and* with FAMINE shall they be consumed in the midst of thee: *and* a third part (1/3) shall fall by the SWORD round about thee; *and* I will SCATTER a third part (1/3) into all the winds, *and* I will draw out a SWORD after them. **THUS SHALL MINE ANGER BE ACCOMPLISHED, and I WILL CAUSE MY FURY TO REST UPON THEM, and** *I WILL BE COMFORTED:* *and* **THEY SHALL KNOW THAT I THE LORD HAVE SPOKEN IT IN MY ZEAL,** *when* **I HAVE ACCOMPLISHED MY FURY IN THEM.** *M-o-r-e-o-v-e-r* **I will make thee WASTE, and a REPROACH among the nations that are round about thee, in the sight of all that pass by. So it shall be a REPROACH and a TAUNT, an INSTRUCTION and an astonishment unto the nations that are round about thee, when I shall execute judgments in thee in ANGER and in FURY and in FURIOUS REBUKES.** I the LORD have spoken it. *When* **I shall send upon them the evil arrows of FAMINE, which shall be for their**

DESTRUCTION, and which I will send TO DESTROY YOU: and I WILL INCREASE THE FAMINE upon you, and will BREAK YOUR STAFF OF BREAD: So will I send upon you FAMINE and EVIL BEASTS, and they shall BEREAVE THEE: and PESTILENCE and BLOOD shall pass through thee; and I will bring the SWORD upon thee. I the LORD have spoken it. (Ezekiel 5:8-17)

And the word of the LORD came unto me, saying, **Son of man, set thy face toward the mountains of Israel, and PROPHESY AGAINST THEM,** And say, YE MOUNTAINS of Israel, hear the word of the Lord GOD; Thus saith the Lord GOD to the MOUNTAINS, and to the HILLS, to the RIVERS, and to the VALLEYS; **Behold, I, even I, will bring a SWORD upon you, and I will DESTROY your high places. And your altars shall be DESOLATE, and your images shall be BROKEN: and I will CAST DOWN your slain men before your idols. And I will lay the DEAD CARCASES of the children of Israel before their idols; and I will SCATTER your bones round about your altars. In all your dwelling places the cities shall be LAID WASTE, and the high places shall be DESOLATE; that your altars may be LAID WASTE and made DESOLATE, and your idols may be BROKEN and CEASE, and your images may be CUT DOWN, and your works may be ABOLISHED. And the SLAIN shall fall in the midst of you, and ye shall know that I am the LORD.** *Yet will I leave a REMNANT, that ye may have some that shall ESCAPE the sword among the nations, when ye shall be scattered through the countries.* ***And they that*** *escape of you shall remember me among the* *nations* *whither they shall be carried captives,* **b-e-c-a-u-s-e** **I AM BROKEN WITH THEIR WHORISH HEART,** which hath departed from me, and with their eyes, which **GO A WHORING AFTER THEIR IDOLS:** *and*

THEY SHALL

L-O-T-H-E T-H-E-M-S-E-L-V-E-S

FOR THE EVILS WHICH T-H-E-Y HAVE COMMITTED IN ALL THEIR ABOMINATIONS. *And they shall know that I am the LORD,* and that **I HAVE** *N-O-T* **SAID IN VAIN THAT I WOULD DO THIS EVIL UNTO THEM.** (Ezekiel 6:1-10)

They have blown the trumpet, even to make all ready; *but* none goeth to the battle: **FOR MY WRATH IS UPON ALL THE MULTITUDE THEREOF.** The SWORD is without, and the PESTILENCE and the FAMINE within: he that is in the field shall die with the SWORD; and he that is in the city, FAMINE and PESTILENCE shall devour him. *But they that* ***escape*** *of them shall escape, and shall be on the mountains like doves of the valleys,* ***all of them mourning, every one for his iniquity.*** All hands shall be feeble, and all knees shall be weak as water. They shall also gird themselves with SACKCLOTH, and HORROR shall cover them; and SHAME shall be upon all faces, and BALDNESS upon all their heads. They shall cast their silver in the streets, and their gold shall be removed: their silver and their gold shall not be able to deliver them in **THE DAY OF THE WRATH OF THE LORD:** they shall not satisfy their souls, neither fill their bowels: because it is the stumblingblock of their INIQUITY.   As for the beauty of his ornament, he set it in majesty: *but* **THEY MADE THE IMAGES OF THEIR ABOMINATIONS and OF THEIR <u>D-E-T-E-S-T-A-B-L-E</u> THINGS THEREIN:** therefore have I set it far from them.   And I will give it into the hands of the strangers for a prey, and to the wicked of the earth for a spoil; and they shall pollute it.   **MY FACE WILL I TURN ALSO FROM THEM,** and they shall pollute my secret place: for the ROBBERS shall enter into it, and defile it.   Make a chain: for the land is full of BLOODY CRIMES, and the city is full of VIOLENCE.   *Wherefore* **I WILL BRING THE <u>WORST</u> OF THE HEATHEN,** and they shall possess their houses: I will also make the POMP of the strong to <u>cease</u>; and their holy places shall be defiled. DESTRUCTION cometh; and they shall seek peace, and there shall be NONE.   **<u>MISCHIEF shall come upon MISCHIEF</u>**, and **<u>RUMOUR shall be upon RUMOUR</u>;** then shall they seek a vision of the prophet; but the law shall perish from the priest, and counsel from the ancients.   The king shall MOURN, and the prince shall be clothed with DESOLATION, and the hands of the people of the land shall be troubled: **I WILL DO UNTO THEM AFTER T-H-E-I-R WAY, and ACCORDING TO T-H-E-I-R DESERTS (DESERVED PUNISHMENT) WILL I JUDGE THEM; and <u>they shall know that I am the LORD</u>.** (Ezekiel 7:14-27)

Therefore say, Thus saith the Lord GOD; *Although* I have CAST THEM FAR OFF among the heathen, and although I have SCATTERED them among the countries, *yet will I be to them as a little sanctuary in the countries where they shall come.* Therefore say, Thus saith the Lord GOD; I will even gather you from the people, and assemble you out of the countries where ye have been scattered, and I WILL GIVE YOU THE LAND OF ISRAEL. And they shall come thither, and **they shall take away** *all* **the DETESTABLE things thereof and** *all* **the ABOMINATIONS thereof from thence.** *And I will give them* <u>*one heart,*</u> *and I will put a* <u>*new spirit*</u> *within you; and I will take the stony heart out of their flesh, and will* <u>*give them an heart of flesh*</u>*: That they may walk in my statutes, and keep mine ordinances, and do them: and* **they shall be** <u>**my**</u> **people, and I will be** <u>**their**</u> **God. B-u-t as for them whose heart walketh after the heart of their DETESTABLE THINGS and their a-b-o-m-i-n-a-t-i-o-n-s, I will RECOMPENSE their way upon their** *own* **heads, saith the Lord GOD.** (Ezekiel 11:16-21)

Thou hast borne thy **lewdness** and thine **abominations,** saith the LORD. For thus saith the Lord GOD; **I WILL EVEN DEAL WITH THEE AS THOU HAST DONE, WHICH HAST** <u>**D-E-S-P-I-S-E-D**</u> **THE OATH IN BREAKING THE COVENANT.** *Nevertheless* I will remember *my* covenant with thee in the days of thy youth, and I will establish unto thee an everlasting covenant. ***Then*** thou shalt remember thy ways, and be ASHAMED, when thou shalt receive thy sisters, thine elder and thy younger: and I will give them unto thee for daughters, but not by thy covenant.

And I will establish my covenant with thee; and thou shalt know that I am the LORD: THAT THOU MAYEST **REMEMBER,** and BE **CONFOUNDED,** and NEVER OPEN THY MOUTH ANY MORE BECAUSE OF THY SHAME, <u>**WHEN I AM PACIFIED TOWARD THEE FOR ALL THAT THOU HAST DONE**</u>, saith the Lord GOD. (Ezekiel 16:58-63)

But **THE HOUSE OF ISRAEL R-E-B-E-L-L-E-D AGAINST ME IN THE WILDERNESS: THEY WALKED (LIVED) NOT IN MY STATUTES, and THEY <u>D-E-S-P-I-S-E-D</u> MY JUDGMENTS,** which if a man do, he shall even live in them; and my SABBATHS they *greatly* polluted: then I said, **I WOULD POUR OUT MY <u>FURY</u> UPON THEM IN THE WILDERNESS, TO CONSUME THEM.** *But* I wrought for my name's sake, that <u>IT SHOULD NOT BE POLLUTED BEFORE THE HEATHEN</u>, in whose sight I brought them out. *Yet* also I lifted up my hand unto them in the wilderness, that I WOULD NOT BRING THEM INTO THE LAND WHICH I HAD GIVEN THEM, flowing with milk and honey, which is the glory of all lands; ***B-e-c-a-us-e* they <u>D-E-S-P-I-S-E-D</u> MY JUDGMENTS,** *and* **WALKED (LIVED) <u>NOT</u> IN MY STATUTES,** *but* **POLLUTED MY SABBATHS:** *for* **THEIR HEART WENT AFTER THEIR IDOLS.** *Nevertheless* mine eye spared them from destroying them, *neither* did I make an end of them in the wilderness. *But* I said unto their children in the wilderness, **WALK YE NOT IN THE STATUTES OF YOUR FATHERS, neither observe their judgments, nor defile yourselves with their idols:** I am the LORD your God; WALK IN *<u>MY</u>* STATUTES, *and* KEEP

MY JUDGMENTS, and DO THEM*;* *And* HALLOW *MY* SABBATHS; and they shall be a sign between me and you, that ye may know that I am the LORD your God. *Notwithstanding* **THE CHILDREN REBELLED AGAINST ME: THEY WALKED (LIVED) NOT IN *MY* STATUTES,** *neither* **KEPT *MY* STATUTES,** *neither* **KEPT *MY* JUDGMENTS TO DO THEM,** which *if* a man do, he shall even live in them; **THEY POLLUTED *MY* SABBATHS: then I SAID, I WOULD POUR OUT *MY* FURY UPON THEM, TO ACCOMPLISH *MY* ANGER AGAISNT THEM IN THE WILDERNESS.** *Nevertheless* I withdrew mine hand, and wrought *for my name's sake,* that it should not be polluted in the sight of the heathen, in whose sight I brought them forth. I lifted up mine hand unto them also in the wilderness, that I would scatter them among the heathen, and disperse them through the countries*;* *Because* **THEY HAD NOT EXECUTED *MY* JUDGMENTS,** *but* **HAD D-E-S-P-I-S-E-D *MY* STATUTES,** *and* **HAD POLLUTED *MY* SABBATHS,** *and* **THEIR EYES WERE AFTER THEIR FATHERS' IDOLS.** *Wherefore* I gave them also statutes that were **not** good, **and judgments whereby they should *not* live;** (Ezekiel 20:13-25)

As I live, saith the Lord GOD, surely with a mighty hand, and with a stretched out arm, and **WITH FURY POURED OUT, WILL I RULE OVER YOU:** And I will bring you out from the people, and will gather you out of the countries wherein ye are SCATTERED, with a mighty hand, and with a stretched out arm, and **WITH FURY POURED OUT.** And I will bring you *into* the

WILDERNESS of the people, and **there will I** ***plead* with you face to face.** **Like as I *pleaded* with your fathers in the wilderness of the land of Egypt, so will I *plead* with you, saith the Lord GOD.** And I will cause you to pass under the rod, *and* I *W-I-L-L* BRING YOU INTO THE BOND OF THE COVENANT: *And* I *W-I-L-L* PURGE OUT FROM AMONG YOU THE REBELS, *and* THEM THAT TRANSGRESS AGAINST ME: I *W-I-L-L* BRING THEM FORTH OUT OF THE COUNTRY WHERE THEY SOJOURN, *and* they shall **not** enter into the land of Israel: and YE *S-H-A-L-L* KNOW THAT I AM THE LORD. As for you, O house of Israel, thus saith the Lord GOD; Go ye, serve ye every one his idols, and hereafter also, if ye will not hearken unto me: **but *pollute ye my holy name no more*** with your gifts, and with your idols. For in mine holy mountain, in the mountain of the height of Israel, saith the Lord GOD, there shall *all* the house of Israel, *all* of them in the land, SERVE ME: *there will I accept them, and there will I require your offerings, and the firstfruits of your oblations, with all your holy things. I will accept you with your sweet savour, when I bring you **out** from the people, and gather you **out** of the countries wherein ye have been scattered; and I will be sanctified in you before the heathen. And ye shall know that I am the LORD, when I shall bring you into the land of Israel, into the country for the which I lifted up mine hand to give it to your fathers.* And *t-h-e-r-e* **shall ye r-e-m-e-m-b-e-r your ways, and *all* your doings, wherein ye have been DEFILED**; *and*

Y-E S-H-A-L-L

66

L-O-T-H-E Y-O-U-R-S-E-L-V-E-S

IN YOUR *OWN* SIGHT FOR ALL YOUR EVILS THAT YE HAVE COMMITTED. And ye shall know that I am the LORD when I have wrought with you for my name's sake, ***not*** **according to your wicked ways, *nor* according to your corrupt doings,** O ye house of Israel, saith the Lord GOD. (Ezekiel 20:33-44)

Thou hast D-E-S-P-I-S-E-D mine holy things, and hast PROFANED my SABBATHS. (Ezekiel 22:8)

And when **they entered unto the heathen,** whither they went, **THEY PROFANED MY HOLY NAME,** when they said to them, These are the people of the LORD, and are gone forth out of his land.

B-u-t

I HAD PITY FOR

M-I-N-E

HOLY NAME,

which the house of Israel had PROFANED among the heathen, whither they went. Therefore say unto the house of Israel, thus saith the Lord GOD; **I do NOT this for *your* sakes, O house of Israel, but FOR M-I-N-E HOLY NAME'S SAKE,** which *ye* have PROFANED among the heathen, whither ye went.   And **I W-I-L-L SANCTIFY** *MY* **GREAT NAME,** which was profaned among the heathen, which ye have profaned in the midst of them; ***and the heathen shall know that I am the*** L*ORD,* saith the Lord G*OD,* ***when I shall be sanctified in you before their eyes.***   *For* I will take you from among the heathen, and gather you out of all countries, and will BRING YOU INTO YOUR OWN LAND. Then will I sprinkle clean water upon you, and ye shall be clean: from all your FILTHINESS, and from all your idols, will I cleanse you. *A new heart also will **I** give you, and a new spirit will **I** put within you: and **I** will take away the stony heart out of your flesh, and **I** will give you an heart of flesh. And **I** will put **my spirit** within you, and cause you to walk in **my statutes**, and ye shall keep **my judgments**, and do them. And ye shall dwell in the land that **I** gave to your fathers; and ye shall be **my people**, and **I** will be your God. **I will also save you from all YOUR UNCLEANNESSES**:* and I will call for the corn, and will increase it, and lay no famine upon you.   And I will multiply the fruit of the tree, and the increase of the field, that ye shall receive no more reproach of famine among the heathen. ***T-h-e-n* SHALL YE REMEMBER YOUR O-W-N EVIL WAYS, and Y-O-U-R DOINGS THAT WERE NOT GOOD, and SHALL**

L-O-T-H-E Y-O-U-R-S-E-L-V-E-S

IN YOUR OWN SIGHT FOR YOUR INIQUITIES and FOR YOUR ABOMINATIONS.   **Not for *your* sakes do I this,** saith the Lord G*OD,* be it known unto you: **BE ASHAMED and CONFOUNDED FOR YOUR OWN WAYS,** O house of Israel.   Thus saith the

Lord GOD; *In the day that I shall have cleansed you from all your iniquities I* will also cause you to dwell in the cities, and the wastes shall be builded. And the desolate land shall be tilled, whereas it lay desolate in the sight of all that passed by. And they shall say, *This land that was desolate is become like the garden of Eden; and the waste and desolate and ruined cities are become fenced, and are inhabited.* *T-h-e-n* <u>the heathen that are left round about you shall know that *"I the LORD"* build the ruined places, and plant that that was desolate:</u> *I* the LORD have spoken it, and *I* will do it. Thus saith the Lord GOD; *I* will yet for this be enquired of by the house of Israel, to do it for them; *I* will increase them with men like a flock. As the holy flock, as the flock of Jerusalem in her solemn feasts; so shall the waste cities be filled with flocks of men: *and* **THEY SHALL KNOW THAT *I* AM THE LORD.** (Ezekiel 36:20-38)

And say unto them, *Thus saith the Lord GOD; Behold, I will take the children of Israel from among the heathen, whither they be gone, and will gather them on every side, and <u>bring them into their own land</u>: And I will make them one nation in the land upon the mountains of Israel; and one king shall be king to them all: and they shall be no more two nations, neither shall they be divided into two kingdoms any more at all.* **Neither** *shall they* **DEFILE THEMSELVES any more with their idols,** *nor* **with their <u>DETESTABLE</u> things,** *nor* **with any of their transgressions:** *but I will save them out of all their dwellingplaces, wherein they have sinned, and* **will cleanse them:** *so shall they be* **my** *people, and I will be their God. And David* **my** *servant shall be king over them; and they all shall* *have one shepherd: they shall also walk in **my** JUDGMENTS, and observe **my** STATUTES, and do them. And they shall dwell in the land that **I** have given unto Jacob my servant, wherein your fathers have dwelt; and they shall dwell therein, even they, and their children, and their children's children for ever: and **my** servant David shall be their prince for ever. **M-o-r-e-o-v-e-r** I will make a COVENANT OF PEACE with them; it shall be an EVERLASTING COVENANT with them: and **I** will place them, and multiply them, and will set **my** sanctuary in the midst of them for evermore. **My** tabernacle also shall be with them: yea, **I** will be their God, and they shall be **my** people. And the heathen shall know that **I** the LORD do sanctify Israel, when **my** sanctuary shall be in the midst of them for evermore.* (Ezekiel 37:21-28)

All their wickedness is in Gilgal: *for* **there I H-A-T-E-D T-H-E-M: for THE WICKEDNESS OF THEIR DOINGS I will drive them out of mine house, I WILL LOVE THEM** *NO* **MORE: all their princes are revolters.** (Hosea 9:15)

Thus saith the LORD; For THREE transgressions of Judah, and for FOUR, I will not turn away the punishment thereof; *b-e-c-a-u-s-e* **THEY HAVE D-E-S-P-I-S-E-D THE LAW OF THE LORD,** *and* **HAVE NOT KEPT HIS COMMANDMENTS, and THEIR LIES CAUSED THEM TO ERR,** after the which their *fathers* have walked: (Amos 2:4)

THEY H-A-T-E HIM THAT REBUKETH IN THE GATE, and THEY A-B-H-O-R HIM THAT SPEAKETH UPRIGHTLY. Forasmuch

70

therefore as **your treading is upon the poor,** *and* **ye take from him burdens of wheat: ye have built houses of hewn stone,** *but* ye shall NOT dwell in them; ye have planted pleasant vineyards, *but* ye shall NOT drink wine of them. *For* **I KNOW YOUR MANIFOLD TRANSGRESSIONS and YOUR MIGHTY SINS: THEY (1) AFFLICT THE JUST, (2) THEY TAKE A BRIBE,** *and* **(3) THEY TURN ASIDE THE POOR IN THE GATE FROM THEIR RIGHT.** *Therefore* **the prudent shall keep** *silence* **in that time; for it is an EVIL time.** SEEK GOOD, and NOT EVIL, THAT YE MAY LIVE: *and so the* LORD, *the God of hosts, shall be with you, as ye have spoken.* **H-A-T-E THE EVIL,** *and* LOVE THE GOOD, *and* ESTABLISH JUDGMENT in the gate: it may be that the LORD God of hosts will be gracious unto the remnant of Joseph. (Amos 5:10-15)

I H-A-T-E, I D-E-S-P-I-S-E YOUR FEAST DAYS, and I will not smell in your solemn assemblies. (Amos 5:21)

The Lord GOD *hath* **sworn by himself,** saith the LORD the God of hosts, **I A-B-H-O-R THE EXCELLENCY OF JACOB, and H-A-T-E HIS PALACES:** *therefore* will I deliver up the city with all that is therein. (Amos 6:8)

And I said, Hear, I pray you, O heads of Jacob, and ye princes of the house of Israel; **Is it not for you to know judgment? WHO H-A-T-E THE GOOD, and LOVE THE EVIL; who pluck off their skin from off them, and their flesh from off their bones; Who also eat the flesh of my people, and**

71

flay their skin from off them; and they break their bones, and chop them in pieces, as for the pot, and as flesh within the caldron. Then shall they (the heads of Jacob) cry unto the LORD, *but* **HE WILL N-O-T HEAR THEM: HE WILL EVEN HIDE HIS FACE FROM THEM AT THAT TIME,** *as* <u>**THEY HAVE BEHAVED THEMSELVES ILL IN THEIR DOINGS**</u>. (Micah 3:1-4)

Hear this, I pray you, ye heads of the house of Jacob, and princes of the house of Israel, **THAT** <u>**A-B-H-O-R**</u> **JUDGMENT, and** <u>**PERVERT**</u> **ALL EQUITY. They build up Zion with BLOOD, and Jerusalem with INIQUITY.** The heads thereof judge for reward, and the priests thereof teach for hire, and the prophets thereof divine for money: *yet* <u>will they lean upon the LORD, and say, Is not the LORD among us? none evil can come upon us</u>. *T-h-e-r-ef-o-r-e* **SHALL ZION** <u>**for your sake**</u> **BE PLOWED AS A FIELD, and JERUSALEM SHALL BECOME HEAPS, and THE MOUNTAIN OF THE HOUSE AS THE HIGH PLACES OF THE FOREST.** (Micah 3:1-12)

And the angel that talked with me came again, and waked me, as a man that is wakened out of his sleep. And said unto me, **What seest thou?** And I said, I have looked, and behold <u>**a CANDLESTICK all of gold,**</u> with a <u>**bowl upon the top**</u> of it, and his <u>**seven lamps**</u> thereon, and <u>**seven pipes**</u> to the seven lamps, which are upon the top thereof: *And* <u>**two OLIVE TREES**</u> by it, <u>one upon the right side</u> of the bowl, and <u>the other upon the left side</u> thereof. So I answered and spake to the angel that talked with me, saying, (Q) *What are these, my lord?*

Then the angel that talked with me answered and said unto me, Knowest thou not what these be? And I said, No, my lord. Then he answered and spake unto me, saying, This is the word of the LORD unto Zerubbabel, saying, (A) *Not by might, nor by power, but by my spirit,* saith the LORD of hosts. Who art thou, O great mountain? before Zerubbabel thou shalt become a plain: and he shall bring forth the headstone thereof with shoutings, crying, Grace, grace unto it. Moreover the word of the LORD came unto me, saying, The hands of Zerubbabel have laid the foundation of this house; his hands shall also finish it; and thou shalt know that the LORD of hosts hath sent me unto you. For who hath **DESPISED** the day of small things? for they shall *rejoice,* and shall see the plummet in the hand of Zerubbabel with those seven; **they are the eyes of the LORD, which run to and fro through the whole earth.** Then answered I, and said unto him, (Q) **What are these two olive trees** upon the right side of the candlestick and upon the left side thereof? And I answered again, and said unto him, (A) What be these TWO OLIVE BRANCHES which through the two golden pipes empty the golden oil out of themselves? And he answered me and said, Knowest thou not what these be? And I said, No, my lord. Then said he, *These are the two anointed ones, that stand by the LORD of the whole earth.* (Zechariah 4:1-14)

Three shepherds also I cut off in one month; and MY SOUL L-O-T-H-E-D THEM, and THEIR SOUL ALSO A-B-H-O-R-R-E-D ME. (Zechariah 11:8)

These are the things that ye shall do; *Speak ye every man the TRUTH to his neighbour; execute the judgment of TRUTH and PEACE in your gates:* **A-n-d LET NONE OF YOU IMAGINE EVIL IN YOUR HEARTS AGAINST HIS NEIGHBOUR; and LOVE NO FALSE OATH: for ALL THESE THINGS THAT I H-A-T-E,** saith the LORD. (Zechariah 8:16-17)

The burden of the word of the LORD to Israel by Malachi. *I have loved you*, saith the LORD. *Yet* ye say, Wherein hast thou loved us? Was not Esau Jacob's brother? saith the LORD: yet *I loved Jacob, And* **I HATED ESAU,** and laid his mountains and his heritage WASTE for the dragons of the wilderness. Whereas Edom saith, We are impoverished, but we will return and build the desolate places; thus saith the LORD of hosts, **"They" shall build,** *but* **"I" will throw down;** and *they* shall call them, **The border of wickedness,** *and,* **The people against whom the LORD hath indignation FOR EVER.** And your eyes shall see, and ye shall say, *The LORD will be magnified from the border of Israel.* A son honoureth his father, and a servant his master: *if* then I be a <u>father,</u> WHERE IS MINE HONOUR? and *if* I be a <u>master,</u> WHERE IS MY FEAR saith the LORD of hosts unto you, **O PRIESTS, THAT D-E-S-P-I-S-E MY NAME.** And ye say, (Q) **Wherein have we DESPISED thy name?** (A) <u>Ye offer polluted bread upon mine altar</u>; and ye say, Wherein have we polluted thee? In that ye say, <u>The table of the LORD is contemptible.</u> **And if ye offer the BLIND for sacrifice, <u>is it not evil?</u> and if ye offer the LAME and SICK, <u>is it not evil?</u>** <u>offer it now unto *thy* governor; will *he* be pleased with thee, or accept *thy*</u>

<u>person</u>? saith the LORD of hosts. And now, I pray you, beseech God that he will be gracious unto us: this hath been by your means: will he regard your persons? saith the LORD of hosts. Who is there even among you that would shut the doors for nought? neither do ye kindle fire on mine altar for nought. **I HAVE NO PLEASURE IN YOU**, saith the LORD of hosts, *neither* <u>will I accept an offering at your hand</u>. For from the rising of the sun even unto the going down of the same ***<u>my name shall be GREAT among the Gentiles</u>; and in every place incense shall be offered unto my name, and a pure offering: <u>for my name shall be GREAT among the heathen</u>,*** saith the LORD of hosts. ***B-u-t* "YE" HAVE PROFANED IT,** in that ye say, The table of the LORD is polluted; and the fruit thereof, even his meat, is **C-O-N-T-E-M-P-T-I-B-L-E.** Ye said also, Behold, what a weariness is it! and ye have snuffed at it, saith the LORD of hosts; and **<u>ye</u> brought that which was TORN, and <u>the LAME</u>, and <u>the SICK</u>;** thus ye brought an offering: **SHOULD I ACCEPT THIS OF YOUR HAND?** saith the LORD. ***But* <u>CURSED</u> BE THE <u>DECEIVER</u>, which hath in his flock a male, and voweth, and sacrificeth unto the LORD a CORRUPT THING: for I am a great King, saith the LORD of hosts, and MY NAME IS <u>DREADFUL</u> AMONG THE HEATHEN.** (Malichi 1:1-14)

Judah hath dealt TREACHEROUSLY, and an ABOMINATION is committed in Israel and in Jerusalem; for Judah hath PROFANED the holiness of the LORD which he loved, and hath married the daughter of a STRANGE GOD. THE LORD WILL <u>CUT OFF</u> THE MAN

THAT DOETH THIS, the master and the scholar, out of the tabernacles of Jacob, and him that offereth an offering unto the LORD of hosts. **And this have ye done** *again,* covering the altar of the LORD with tears, with weeping, and with crying out, insomuch that he regardeth not the offering any more, or receiveth it with good will at your hand. Yet ye say, **WHEREFORE?** *B-e-c-a-u-s-e* **THE LORD HATH BEEN WITNESS BETWEEN THEE and THE WIFE OF THY YOUTH, AGAINST WHOM THOU HAST DEALT TREACHEROUSLY: YET IS SHE THY COMPANION, and THE WIFE OF THY COVENANT.** And did not he make one? Yet had he the residue of the spirit. **(Q) And wherefore one? (A)** *That he might seek a godly seed. T-h-e-r-e-f-o-r-e* **TAKE HEED TO YOUR SPIRIT, and LET NONE DEAL TREACHEROUSLY AGAINST THE WIFE OF HIS YOUTH.** *For* **THE LORD, THE GOD OF ISRAEL, SAITH THAT HE H-A-T-E-T-H PUTTING AWAY (DIVORCE):** *for* **one covereth violence with his garment, saith the** LORD **of hosts:** *therefore* **TAKE HEED to your spirit, THAT YE DEAL NOT TREACHEROUSLY. Ye have wearied the** LORD **with your words.** Yet *ye* say, **(Q) Wherein have we wearied him? (A) When ye say, EVERY ONE THAT DOETH EVIL IS GOOD IN THE SIGHT OF THE LORD, and he delighteth in them;** *or,* **WHERE IS THE GOD OF JUDGMENT?** (Malachi 2:11-17)

76

NEW TESTAMENT

Ye have heard that it hath been said, **Thou shalt love thy neighbour, and h-a-t-e thine enemy.** *B-u-t* I say unto you, *LOVE YOUR ENEMIES, BLESS THEM THAT CURSE YOU, DO GOOD TO THEM THAT HATE YOU, and PRAY FOR THEM WHICH DESPITEFULLY USE YOU, and PERSECUTE YOU; That ye may be the children of your Father which is in heaven: for he maketh his sun to rise on the evil AND on the good, and sendeth rain on the just AND on the unjust.* **FOR IF YE LOVE THEM WHICH LOVE YOU, WHAT REWARD HAVE YE? do not even the publicans the same?** *And* **IF YE SALUTE YOUR BRETHREN ONLY, WHAT DO YE MORE THAN OTHERS?** *Be ye therefore p-e-r-f-e-c-t, even as your Father which is in heaven is p-e-r-f-e-c-t.* (Matthew 5:43-48)

Lay *not* **up for yourselves treasures upon earth, where moth and rust doth corrupt, and where thieves break through and steal:** *But lay up for yourselves* *treasures in heaven, where neither moth nor rust doth corrupt, and where thieves do not break through nor steal:* FOR WHERE YOUR TREASURE IS, THERE WILL YOUR HEART BE ALSO. *The light of the body is the eye: if therefore thine eye be single, thy whole body shall be full of light.* *But* **if thine eye be EVIL, thy whole body shall be FULL OF DARKNESS. If therefore the**

light that is in thee be darkness, how GREAT is that darkness!

NO MAN CAN SERVE TWO MASTERS:

FOR EITHER HE WILL H-A-T-E THE ONE,

and

LOVE THE OTHER;

or else

HE WILL HOLD TO THE ONE,

and

D-E-S-P-I-S-E THE OTHER.

YE CANNOT SERVE GOD and MAMMON

($$$)

(Matthew 6:19-24)

Behold, I send you forth as sheep in the midst of WOLVES: *be ye therefore wise as serpents, and harmless as doves.* *But* BEWARE OF MEN: for they will deliver you up to the councils, and they will SCOURGE you in their synagogues; And ye shall be brought before governors and kings for my sake, for a testimony against them and the Gentiles. But *when* they deliver you up, take no thought how or what ye shall speak: for it shall be given you in that same hour what ye shall speak. -For it is not ye that speak, but the Spirit of your Father which speaketh in you. **And the <u>BROTHER SHALL DELIVER UP THE BROTHER</u> to DEATH, and the <u>FATHER THE CHILD</u>: and the <u>CHILDREN SHALL RISE UP AGAINST THEIR PARENTS</u>, and cause them to be put to DEATH. *A-n-d* YE SHALL BE <u>H-A-T-E-D</u> OF ALL MEN FOR MY NAME'S SAKE:** *but he that <u>ENDURETH TO THE END</u> shall be SAVED.* (Matthew 10:16-22)

And Jesus went out, and departed from the temple: and his disciples came to him for to shew him the buildings of the temple. And Jesus said unto them, See ye not all these things? verily I say unto you, <u>There shall not be left here one stone upon another, that shall not be thrown down</u>. And as he sat upon the mount of Olives, the disciples came unto him privately, saying, (Q) <u>Tell us, when shall these things be? and what shall be the sign of thy coming, and of the end of the world</u>? And Jesus answered and said unto them, (A) **Take heed that** *no* **man DECEIVE you. For** *m-a-n-y* **shall come in my name, saying, I am Christ; and shall DECEIVE many.** And ye shall hear of wars and rumours of wars: see that ye be *not* troubled: for all these things *m-u-s-t* come to pass, *but* the end is not yet. For <u>nation shall rise against nation</u>, and <u>kingdom against kingdom</u>: and there shall be <u>famines,</u> and <u>pestilences,</u> and <u>earthquakes,</u> in divers places. All these are the *beginning* of sorrows. ***Then* SHALL THEY DELIVER YOU UP TO BE AFFLICTED, and SHALL KILL YOU, and YE SHALL BE <u>H-A-T-E-D</u> OF ALL NATIONS FOR MY NAME'S SAKE. And then shall many be OFFENDED, and shall BETRAY one another, and shall <u>H-A-T-E</u> ONE ANOTHER.**

79

And *m-a-n-y* <u>false prophets</u> shall rise, and shall DECEIVE many. And *because* <u>iniquity shall abound</u>, THE LOVE OF MANY SHALL WAX COLD. *B-u-t <u>he that shall ENDURE UNTO THE END, the same shall be SAVED</u>.* And this gospel of the kingdom shall be preached in *all* the world for a witness unto all nations; and *then* shall the end come. (Matthew 24:1-14)

And as he went out of the temple, one of his disciples saith unto him, Master, see what manner of stones and what buildings are here! And Jesus answering said unto him, Seest thou these great buildings? <u>there shall not be left one stone upon another, that shall not be thrown down</u>. And as he sat upon the mount of Olives over against the temple, Peter and James and John and Andrew asked him privately, (Q) <u>Tell us, when shall these things be? and what shall be the sign when all these things shall be fulfilled</u>? And Jesus answering them began to say, (A) **Take heed lest *any* man deceive you: For *many* shall come in my name, saying, I am Christ; and shall DECEIVE many.** And when ye shall hear of wars and rumours of wars, be ye not troubled: for such things must needs be; *but* the end shall not be yet. <u>For nation shall rise against nation</u>, and <u>kingdom against kingdom</u>: and there shall be <u>earthquakes in divers places</u>, and there shall be <u>famines</u> and <u>troubles</u>: these are the *beginnings* of sorrows. But take heed to yourselves: for they shall deliver you up to councils; and in the synagogues ye shall be BEATEN: and ye shall be brought before rulers and kings for my sake, for a testimony against them. And the gospel must first be published among *all* nations. But when they shall lead you, and deliver you up, take no thought beforehand what ye shall speak, neither do ye premeditate: *but* whatsoever shall be given you in that hour, that speak ye: for it is not ye that speak, but the Holy Ghost. **Now the BROTHER SHALL BETRAY THE BROTHER TO DEATH, and the FATHER THE SON; and CHILDREN SHALL RISE UP AGAINST THEIR PARENTS, and shall cause them to be PUT TO DEATH.** *And* **YE SHALL BE H-A-T-E-D OF ALL MEN FOR MY NAME'S SAKE:** *but he that shall ENDURE UNTO THE END, the same shall be SAVED.* (Mark 13:1-13)

And he lifted up his eyes on his disciples, and said, Blessed be ye POOR: *for yours is the kingdom of God.* Blessed are ye that HUNGER now: *for ye shall be filled.* Blessed are ye that WEEP now: *for ye shall laugh.* **Blessed are ye, when men shall H-A-T-E you, and when they shall separate you from their company, and shall reproach you, and cast out your name as evil, for the Son of man's sake.** *Rejoice ye in that day, and leap for joy: for, behold, your reward is GREAT in heaven: for in the like manner did their fathers unto the prophets.* **But WOE unto you that are RICH! for ye have received your consolation. WOE unto you that are FULL! for ye shall hunger. WOE unto you that LAUGH now! for ye shall mourn and weep. WOE unto you, when all men shall SPEAK WELL OF YOU! for so did their fathers to the *false* prophets.** But I say unto you which hear,

LOVE YOUR ENEMIES,

DO GOOD TO THEM WHICH H-A-T-E YOU,

81

-BLESS THEM THAT CURSE YOU,

a-n-d

PRAY FOR THEM WHICH

D-E-S-P-I-T-E-F-U-L-L-Y

USE YOU.

And <u>unto him that smiteth thee on the one cheek</u> OFFER ALSO THE OTHER; and <u>him that taketh away thy cloak</u> FORBID NOT TO TAKE THY COAT ALSO. GIVE TO EVERY MAN THAT ASKETH OF THEE; *and* <u>of him that taketh away thy goods</u> ASK THEM NOT AGAIN. *And as ye would that men should do to you, do ye also to them l-i-k-e-w-i-s-e.* <u>For *if* ye love them which love you, WHAT THANK HAVE YE?</u> for sinners also love those that love them. <u>And *if* ye do good to them which do good to you, WHAT THANK HAVE YE?</u> for s-i-n-n-e-r-s also do even the same. <u>And *if* ye lend to them of whom ye hope to receive, WHAT THANK HAVE YE?</u> for sinners also lend to sinners, to receive as much again.

B-u-t

LOVE YE YOUR ENEMIES,

and

DO GOOD,

and

LEND, HOPING FOR NOTHING AGAIN;

and

YOUR REWARD SHALL BE GREAT,

and

YE SHALL BE THE CHILDREN OF THE

HIGHEST:

for

he is kind unto the UNTHANKFUL

and to the EVIL.

BE YE THEREFORE MERCIFUL,

AS YOUR FATHER ALSO IS MERCIFUL.

JUDGE NOT, and ye shall not be judged: CONDEMN NOT, and ye shall not be condemned: FORGIVE, and ye shall be forgiven: GIVE, and it shall be given unto you; *good measure, pressed down, and shaken together, and running over, shall men give into your bosom.* **FOR WITH THE SAME MEASURE THAT YE METE WITHAL IT SHALL BE MEASURED TO YOU AGAIN.** (Luke 6:20-38)

He that heareth you heareth me; **and HE THAT D-E-S-P-I-S-E-T-H YOU D-E-S-P-I-S-E-T-H ME; and HE THAT D-E-S-P-I-S-E-T-H ME**

D-E-S-P-I-S-E-T-H HIM THAT SENT ME. (Luke 10:16)

And there went great multitudes with him: and he turned, and said unto them, If any man come to me, and **H-A-T-E** *not* his FATHER, and MOTHER, and WIFE, and CHILDREN, and BRETHREN, and SISTERS, yea, and HIS OWN LIFE ALSO, **HE CANNOT BE MY DISCIPLE**. And whosoever doth *not* **bear his cross, and come after me, CANNOT BE MY DISCIPLE**. *For* which of you, intending to BUIILD A TOWER, sitteth *not* down first, and **COUNTETH THE COST,** whether he have sufficient to finish it? Lest haply, after he hath laid the foundation, and is not able to finish it, all that behold it begin to **MOCK** him, Saying, This man began to build, and was not able to finish. *Or* what KING, GOING TO MAKE WAR against another king, sitteth not down first, and consulteth whether he be able with ten thousand to meet him that cometh against him with twenty thousand? *Or else,* while the other is yet a great way off, he sendeth an ambassage, and desireth conditions of peace. SO LIKEWISE,

WHOSOEVER HE BE OF YOU THAT FORSAKETH NOT

A-L-L

THAT HE HATH, HE CANNOT BE MY DISCIPLE.

Salt is good: *but* if the salt have lost his savour, wherewith shall it be seasoned? **It is neither fit for the land, nor yet for the dunghill; *but* MEN CAST IT OUT.** He that hath ears to hear, LET HIM HEAR. (Luke 14:25-35)

He that is faithful in that which is LEAST is faithful also in MUCH: ***and*** **he that is unjust in the LEAST is unjust also in MUCH.** *If* therefore ye have ***not*** been faithful in the UNRIGHTEOUS MANNON (MATERIAL THINGS), WHO WILL COMMIT TO YOUR TRUST THE TRUE RICHES (SPIRITUAL THINGS)? <u>And if ye have not been faithful in that which is *another man's,* who shall give you that which is *your own?*</u>

NO SERVANT CAN SERVE TWO MASTERS:

for either

HE WILL <u>H-A-T-E</u> THE ONE,

and

LOVE THE OTHER,

or else

HE WILL HOLD TO THE ONE, *and*

<u>D-E-S-P-I-S-E</u> THE OTHER.

YE CANNOT SERVE GOD and MAMMON.

($$$$$$$$$$$$$$$$$$$$$$$$$$$$$$$$$$$$$$$)

(Luke 16:10-13)

And he spake this parable unto certain which trusted in themselves that they were righteous, *and* **D-E-S-P-I-S-E-D OTHERS:** Two men went up into the temple to pray; the one a PHARISEE, and the other a PUBLICAN. The **PHARISEE** stood and prayed thus with himself, God, I thank thee, that I am not as other men are, extortioners, unjust, adulterers, or even as this publican. I fast twice in the week, I give tithes of all that I possess. And the **PUBLICAN,** standing afar off, *would not lift up so much as his eyes unto heaven,* but smote upon his breast, saying, GOD BE MERCIFUL TO ME A SINNER. *I tell you, this man (the publican) went down to his house justified rather than the other:* for every one that **EXALTETH himself shall be ABASED;** *and he that* **HUMBLETH himself shall be EXALTED.** (Luke 18:9-14)

And as they heard these things, he added and spake a parable, because he was nigh to Jerusalem, and *because* they thought that the kingdom of God should IMMEDIATELY appear. He said therefore, "A certain nobleman went into a far country to receive for himself a kingdom, and to return." And he called his TEN SERVANTS, and delivered them ten pounds, and said unto them, OCCUPY TILL I COME. *B-u-t* **HIS CITIZENS H-A-T-E-D HIM,** and sent a message after him, saying, **We will** *not* **have this man to reign over us.** And it came to pass, that when he was returned, having received the kingdom, then he commanded these servants to be called unto him, to whom he had given the money, *that he might know how much every man* *had gained by trading.* Then came the FIRST, saying, Lord, thy <u>pound</u> hath gained TEN pounds. And he said unto him, ***Well, thou good servant: b-e-c-a-u-s-e thou hast been faithful in a very little, have thou authority over ten cities.*** And the SECOND came, saying, Lord, thy <u>pound</u> hath gained FIVE pounds. And he said likewise to him, ***Be thou also over five cities.*** And another came, saying, Lord, behold, here is thy <u>pound</u>, which I have kept laid up in a napkin: <u>For I feared thee, because THOU ART AN AUSTERE MAN: thou takest up that thou layedst not down, and reapest that thou didst not sow.</u> And he saith unto him,

<u>OUT OF THINE OWN MOUTH</u>

WILL I JUDGE THEE,

THOU W-I-C-K-E-D SERVANT.

<u>THOU KNEWEST THAT I WAS AN</u>

<u>AUSTERE MAN,</u>

TAKING UP THAT I LAID NOT DOWN,

and

REAPING THAT I DID NOT SOW:

Wherefore then gavest not thou my money into the bank, that at my coming I might have required mine own with usury? And he said unto them that stood by, **Take from him the pound, and give it to him that hath ten pounds.** (And they said unto him, Lord, he hath ten pounds.) For I say unto you, ***That*** *unto every one which hath shall be given; a-n-d (b-u-t)* **from him that hath not, even that he hath shall be taken away from him.**

B-u-t

THOSE MINE ENEMIES,

WHICH WOULD NOT THAT I SHOULD

REIGN OVER THEM,

BRING HITHER,

and

S-L-A-Y T-H-E-M B-E-F-O-R-E M-E.

And when he had thus spoken, he went before, ascending up to Jerusalem. (Luke 19:11-28)

And as some spake of the TEMPLE, how it was adorned with goodly stones and gifts, he said, As for these things which ye behold, **the days will come, in the which there shall not be left *one* stone upon another, that shall not be thrown down.** And they asked him, saying, (Q) Master, but when shall these things be? and what sign will there be when these things shall come to pass? And he said, (A) Take heed that ye be not deceived: for *many* shall come in my name, saying, I AM CHRIST; and the time draweth near: GO YE **NOT** THEREFORE AFTER THEM. But when ye shall hear of wars and commotions, be not terrified: for these things must first come to pass; *but* the end is not by and by. Then said he unto them, NATION

SHALL RISE AGAINST NATION, and kingdom against kingdom: And GREAT EARTHQUAKES shall be in divers places, and FAMINES, and PESTILENCES; and FEARFUL SIGHTS and GREAT SIGNS shall there be from heaven. **But before all these, they shall <u>lay their hands on you</u>, and <u>persecute you</u>, delivering you up to the <u>synagogues</u>, and into <u>prisons</u>, being brought before kings and rulers for my name's sake.** And it shall turn to you for a testimony. Settle it therefore in your hearts, *not* to meditate before what ye shall answer: *For I will give you a mouth and wisdom, which all your adversaries shall not be able to gainsay nor resist.* ***A-n-d* YE SHALL BE BETRAYED BOTH BY <u>PARENTS</u>, and <u>BRETHREN</u>, and <u>KINSFOLKS</u>, and <u>FRIENDS</u>; and SOME OF YOU SHALL THEY CAUSE TO BE PUT TO DEATH. *A-n-d* YE SHALL BE <u>H-A-T-E-D</u> OF ALL MEN FOR MY NAME'S SAKE. *B-u-t* there shall not an hair of your head** perish. In your <u>patience possess ye your souls</u>. **And when ye shall see Jerusalem compassed with armies, then know that the desolation thereof is nigh.** (Luke 21:5-20)

<u>*If* I have told you EARTHLY things, and ye believe not, how shall ye believe, *if* I tell you of HEAVENLY things</u>? And no man hath ascended up to heaven, but he that came down from heaven, even THE SON OF MAN which is in heaven. And as Moses lifted up the serpent in the wilderness, even so must the Son of man be lifted up: ***<u>That whosoever believeth in him should not perish, but have eternal life. For God so loved the world, that he gave his only begotten Son, that whosoever believeth in him should not perish, but have</u>***

everlasting life. *For God sent not his Son into the world to condemn the world; but that the world through him might be saved*. *He that believeth on him is not condemned*: *but* **HE THAT BELIEVETH NOT IS CONDEMNED ALREADY,** *because* **HE HATH NOT BELIEVED IN THE NAME OF THE ONLY BEGOTTEN SON OF GOD. And this is the condemnation, that light is come into the world, and MEN LOVED DARKNESS RATHER THAN LIGHT,** *because* **THEIR DEEDS WERE EVIL.** *For* **every one that DOETH EVIL H-A-T-E-T-H THE LIGHT, neither cometh to the light, LEST HIS DEEDS SHOULD BE REPROVED.** *But he that DOETH TRUTH cometh to the light, that his deeds may be made manifest, that they are wrought in God.* (John 3:12-21)

For there is no man that doeth any thing in secret, and he himself seeketh to be known openly. If thou do these things, SHEW THYSELF to the world. **For neither did his brethren believe in him.** Then Jesus said unto them, <u>My time is not yet come</u>: but your time is alway ready. **THE WORLD CANNOT H-A-T-E YOU; but ME IT H-A-T-E-T-H,** *b-e-c-a-u-s-e* **I TESTIFY OF IT, THAT THE WORKS THEREOF ARE E-V-I-L.** (John 7:4-7)

And Jesus answered them, saying, The hour is come, that the Son of man should be glorified. Verily, verily, I say unto you, *Except a corn of wheat fall into the ground and die, it abideth alone: but if it DIE, it bringeth forth MUCH fruit.*

HE THAT <u>L-O-V-E-T</u>-H HIS LIFE SHALL

<u>L-O-S-E</u> <u>I-T</u>;

and HE THAT <u>H-A-T-E-T-H</u> HIS LIFE

IN THIS WORLD SHALL

<u>K-E-E-P</u> <u>I-T</u>

UNTO LIFE ETERNAL.

If any man <u>serve me</u>, let him <u>*follow me*</u>; and where I am, there shall also my servant be: *if* any man SERVE ME, <u>him will my Father honour.</u> (John 12:23-26)

"I" am the true vine, and "my Father" is the husbandman. Every branch in me that beareth *not* fruit HE TAKETH AWAY: *and every branch that beareth fruit, he PURGETH IT, that it may bring forth MORE fruit.* Now ye are clean through the word which I have spoken unto you. *Abide in me, and I in you.* As the branch cannot bear fruit of itself, except it abide in the vine; no more can ye, except ye abide in me. <u>"I" am the VINE, "ye" are the BRANCHES</u>: *He that abideth in me, and I in him, the same bringeth forth MUCH fruit:* for without me ye can do NOTHING. *If* a man abide *not* in me, he is cast forth as a branch, and is withered; and men gather them, and CAST THEM INTO THE FIRE, and they are B-U-R-N-E-D. *If ye abide in me, and my words abide in you, ye shall ask what ye will, and it shall be done unto you. Herein is my Father glorified, that ye BEAR MUCH FRUIT; so shall*

ye be my disciples. <u>As the Father hath loved me, so have I loved you:</u> *continue* ye in my love. *"If"* *ye* **keep my commandments, ye shall abide in my love; even as I have kept my Father's commandments, and abide in his love.** These things have I spoken unto you, that my joy might remain in you, and that your joy might be full. <u>This is my commandment</u>, THAT YE LOVE ONE ANOTHER, AS I HAVE LOVED YOU. <u>Greater love hath no man than this, that a man LAY DOWN HIS LIFE for his friends.</u> *Ye are my friends, "if" ye do whatsoever I command you.* Henceforth I call you not servants; for the servant knoweth not what his lord doeth: *but I have called you FRIENDS; for all things that I have heard of my Father I have made known unto you.* Ye have not chosen me, but I HAVE CHOSEN YOU, and ordained you, that ye should go and ***BRING FORTH FRUIT,*** and that your fruit should REMAIN: *that whatsoever ye shall ask of the Father in my name, he may give it you.* These things I c-o-m-m-a-n-d you, that ye *LOVE ONE ANOTHER.*

If THE "WORLD" <u>H-A-T-E</u> YOU,

YE KNOW THAT IT <u>H-A-T-E-D</u> ME

before IT <u>H-A-T-E-D</u> YOU.

If ye were of the "WORLD," the world would love his own: *b-u-t b-e-c-a-u-s-e* ye are not of the world, *but* **I have chosen you** *out* **of the "world,"**

t-h-e-r-e-f-o-r-e

THE "WORLD" H-A-T-E-T-H YOU.

Remember the word that I said unto you,

The servant is not greater than his lord.

If **THEY HAVE PERSECUTED ME,**

THEY W-I-L-L ALSO PERSECUTE YOU;

if they have kept my saying, they will keep yours also.   But all these things will they do unto you for my name's sake, *because* they know not him that sent me.   *If* **I had not come and spoken unto them, they had not had sin:** *but* **NOW THEY HAVE NO CLOAK (COVERING/EXCUSE) FOR THEIR SIN.**

HE THAT H-A-T-E-T-H ME

H-A-T-E-T-H MY FATHER ALSO.

If I had not done among them the works which none other man did, they had not had sin: *but* **NOW HAVE THEY BOTH SEEN and H-A-T-E-D BOTH ME and MY FATHER.** *But* this cometh to pass, that the word might be fulfilled that is written in their law,

THEY H-A-T-E-D ME WITHOUT A CAUSE.

But when the Comforter is come, whom I will send unto you from the Father, even the Spirit of truth, which proceedeth from the Father, he shall testify of me: And ye also shall bear witness, because ye

have been with me from the beginning. (John 15:1-27)

*These words spake Jesus, and lifted up his eyes to heaven, and said, Father, the hour is come; <u>glorify thy Son, that thy Son also may glorify thee</u>: As thou hast given him POWER OVER ALL FLESH, <u>that he should give eternal life to as many as thou hast given him</u>. And this is LIFE ETERNAL, that they might <u>know thee the only true God</u>, **and** <u>Jesus Christ, whom thou hast sent</u>.* **I have glorified thee on the earth: I have finished the work which thou gavest me to do.** *And now, O Father, glorify thou me with thine own self with the glory which I had with thee before the world was.* **I have manifested thy name unto the men which thou gavest me out of the world:** <u>thine they were</u>, *and* <u>thou gavest them me</u>; *and* <u>they have kept thy word</u>. *Now they have known that all things <u>whatsoever thou hast given me are of thee</u>. For I have given unto them the words which thou gavest me; and they have received them, and have known surely that I came out from thee, and* **they have believed that thou didst send me.** <u>**I pray for them**</u>: *I pray not for the world, but for them which thou hast given me; <u>for they are thine</u>. And all mine are thine, and thine are mine; and I am glorified in them. And now I am no more in the world, but these are in the world, and I come to thee.* <u>**Holy Father, keep through thine own name those whom thou hast given me, that they may be one, as we are.**</u> **While I was with them in the world, I kept them in thy name:** *those that thou gavest me I have kept, and none of them is lost, b-u-t* THE SON OF PERDITION; *that the scripture might be fulfilled. And <u>now come I to thee</u>; and these things I speak in the world,* <u>**that they might**</u>

have my joy fulfilled in themselves. **I have given them thy word;**

and

THE WORLD HATH <u>H-A-T-E-D</u> THEM,

because

THEY ARE N-O-T OF THE WORLD,

EVEN AS I AM N-O-T OF THE WORLD.

*I pray <u>not</u> that thou shouldest take them out of the world, but **that thou shouldest keep them from the evil.** They are **not** of the world, even as I am **not** of the world. **Sanctify them through thy truth: <u>thy WORD is truth.</u>** As thou hast sent me into the world, even so have I also sent them into the world. And for their sakes <u>I sanctify myself,</u> that they also might be sanctified through the truth. **Neither pray I for these alone, but for them <u>also</u> which shall believe on me through their word; <u>That they all may be one; as thou, Father, art in me, and I in thee, that they also may be one in us</u>:** that the world may believe that thou hast sent me. And the glory which thou gavest me I have given them; <u>that they may be one</u>, even as we are one: I in them, and thou in me, that they may be made <u>perfect in one</u>; and that the world may know that thou hast sent me, and hast loved them, as thou hast loved me. Father, I will that they also, whom thou hast given me, be with me where I am; that they may behold my glory, which thou hast given me: for thou lovedst me before the foundation of the world. **O righteous Father,** the "world" hath not known* thee: *b-u-t I have known thee, and these have known that thou hast sent me. And I have declared unto them THY name, and will declare it: that the love wherewith thou hast loved me may be in them, and I in them.* (John 17:1-26)

For I am not ashamed of the gospel of Christ: for it is the power of God unto salvation to every one that believeth; to the Jew first, and also to the Greek. For therein is the righteousness of God revealed from FAITH TO FAITH: as it is written, THE JUST SHALL LIVE BY FAITH. **FOR THE WRATH OF GOD IS REVEALED FROM HEAVEN AGAINST ALL UNGODLINESS *and* UNRIGHTEOUSNESS OF MEN,** who hold the truth in unrighteousness; *B-e-c-a-u-s-e* that which may be known of God is manifest in them; for God hath shewed it unto them. For the invisible things of him from the creation of the world are CLEARLY SEEN, being understood by the things that are made, even his eternal power and Godhead; **SO THAT THEY ARE WITHOUT EXCUSE:** *Because* **that, when they knew God, they glorified him *not* as God, *neither* were thankful; *but* became vain in their imaginations, and their foolish heart was darkened. Professing themselves to be wise, they became FOOLS,** And changed the glory of the uncorruptible God into an image made like to corruptible man, and to birds, and fourfooted beasts, and creeping things.

W-h-e-r-e-f-o-r-e

GOD ALSO GAVE THEM UP

TO UNCLEANNESS THROUGH THE LUSTS OF THEIR OWN HEARTS, TO DISHONOUR THEIR OWN BODIES B-E-T-W-E-E-N T-H-E-M-S-E-L-V-E-S: Who **changed** the truth of God into a **lie,** and worshipped and served the creature more than the Creator, who is blessed for ever. Amen. *For this cause*

GOD GAVE THEM UP

UNTO VILE AFFECTIONS:

for even their *women* did change the natural use into that which is against nature: And likewise also the *men*, leaving the natural use of the woman, BURNED IN THEIR LUST ONE TOWARD ANOTHER; men with men working that which is unseemly, and receiving in themselves that RECOMPENCE of their error which was meet. And even as they did not like to retain God in their knowledge, GOD GAVE THEM OVER TO A REPROBATE MIND, to do those things which are *not* convenient; Being filled with all unrighteousness, fornication, wickedness, covetousness, maliciousness; full of envy, murder, debate, deceit, malignity; whisperers, -Backbiters, HATERS OF GOD, despiteful, proud, boasters, inventors of evil things, disobedient to parents, Without understanding, covenantbreakers, without natural affection, implacable, unmerciful: Who knowing the judgment of God, that THEY WHICH COMMIT SUCH THINGS ARE W-O-R-T-H-Y O-F D-E-A-T-H, not only do the same, but have *pleasure* in them that do them. (Romans 1:16-32)

Therefore **THOU ART I-N-E-X-C-U-S-A-B-L-E, O MAN, whosoever thou art that <u>judgest</u>: for wherein thou <u>judgest</u> another, thou condemnest thyself; for thou that <u>judgest</u> DOEST THE SAME THINGS.** *But* we are sure that the judgment of God is according to truth against them which commit such things. **And thinkest thou this, O man, that judgest them which do such things, and DOEST THE SAME, that thou shalt escape <u>the judgment of God</u>?** *Or* **D-E-S-P-I-S-E-S-T THOU THE RICHES OF HIS GOODNESS and FORBEARANCE and LONGSUFFERING;** *not knowing that the goodness of God leadeth thee to r-r-p-e-n-t-a-n-c-e?* **But AFTER THY <u>HARDNESS</u>** *and* **<u>IMPENITENT HEART</u> TREASUREST UP UNTO THYSELF <u>W-R-A-T-H</u> AGAINST THE DAY OF <u>W-R-A-T-H</u> and REVELATION OF THE RIGHTEOUS JUDGMENT OF GOD; WHO WILL RENDER TO EVERY MAN ACCORDING TO HIS D-E-E-D-S:** *To them who by patient continuance in well doing seek for glory and honour and immortality, <u>eternal life</u>:* **But UNTO THEM THAT ARE CONTENTIOUS,** *and* **DO NOT OBEY THE TRUTH,** *but* **OBEY UNRIGHTEOUSNESS, INDIGNATION** *and* **WRATH, TRIBULATION** *and* **ANGUISH, UPON EVERY SOUL OF MAN THAT D-O-E-T-H EVIL,** of the Jew first, and also of the Gentile; *But glory, honour, and peace, to every man that WORKETH GOOD, to the Jew first, and also to the Gentile: For there is <u>no respect of persons with God</u>.* (Romans 2:1-11)

THOU THEREFORE WHICH TEACHEST ANOTHER, **TEACHEST THOU NOT THYSELF?** thou that preachest a man should not steal, **dost** *thou* **steal?** Thou that sayest a man should not commit adultery, **dost** *thou* **commit adultery?** thou that **ABHORREST IDOLS, dost** *thou* commit **sacrilege?** Thou that makest thy boast of the law, through breaking the law dishonourest thou God? **FOR THE NAME OF GOD IS BLASPHEMED AMONG THE GENTILES THROUGH YOU,** as it is written. For circumcision verily profiteth, *if* **thou keep the LAW:** *but if* thou be a breaker of the law, thy circumcision is made uncircumcision. Therefore if the uncircumcision keep the righteousness of the law, shall not his uncircumcision be counted for circumcision? And shall not uncircumcision which is by nature, if it fulfil the law, judge thee, who by the letter and circumcision dost transgress the law? **For he is** *not* **a Jew, which is one OUTWARDLY; neither is that circumcision, which is outward in the flesh:** *But he is a Jew, which is one INWARDLY; and circumcision is that of the HEART, in the SPIRIT, and not in the letter; whose praise is not of men, but of GOD.* (Romans 2:21-29)

What shall we say then? **Is the law sin? GOD FORBID.** Nay, I had not known sin, but by the law: for I had not known lust, except the law had said, Thou shalt not covet. But sin, taking occasion by the commandment, wrought in me all manner of concupiscence. For without the law sin was dead. For I was alive without the law once: *but* **when the commandment came, sin revived, and I died.** And the commandment, which was ordained to life,

99

I found to be unto death. For SIN, taking occasion by the commandment, DECEIVED ME, and by it SLEW ME. *Wherefore* THE LAW IS HOLY, and THE COMMANDMENT HOLY, and JUST, and GOOD. **Was then that which is good made death unto me? GOD FORBID.** But sin, that it might appear sin, working death in me by that which is good; that sin by the commandment might become *exceeding* **sinful.** For we know that THE LAW IS SPIRITUAL: *but* **I am carnal,** sold under sin. For that which I do I allow not: for what I would, that do I not; but what I **HATE**, that do I. If then I do that which I would not, I consent unto the law that it is good. Now then it is no more I that do it, *but* **SIN THAT DWELLETH IN ME. For I know that in me (that is, in my flesh,) dwelleth NO GOOD THING:** for to will is present with me; but how to perform that which is good I find not. For the good that I would I DO NOT: *but* the evil which I would not, THAT I DO. Now if I do that I would not, it is no more I that do it, *but* SIN THAT DWELLETH IN ME. I find then a law, that, when I would do good, EVIL IS PRESENT WITH ME. For I delight in the law of God after the inward man: *But* **I see another law in my members, WARRING against the law of my mind,** and bringing me into captivity to the law of sin which is in my members. **O wretched man that I am**! who shall deliver me from the body of this death? I thank God through Jesus Christ our Lord. **So then with the mind I myself SERVE THE LAW of God;** *but* **with the flesh the LAW OF SIN.** (Romans 7:1-25)

Let love be without dissimulation. **A-B-H-O-R THAT WHICH IS EVIL**; *cleave to that which is* *good.* Be kindly affectioned one to another with brotherly love; in honour preferring one another; *Not* slothful in business; fervent in spirit; serving the Lord; Rejoicing in hope; patient in tribulation; continuing instant in prayer; Distributing to the necessity of saints; given to hospitality.

BLESS THEM WHICH PERSECUTE YOU:

BLESS, *and* CURSE NOT.

Rejoice with them that do rejoice, and weep with them that weep. Be of the same mind one toward another. Mind not high things, *but* condescend to men of low estate. Be not wise in your own conceits. **RECOMPENSE TO NO MAN EVIL FOR EVIL.** Provide things honest in the sight of all men. If it be possible, as much as lieth in you, live peaceably with all men. Dearly beloved,

AVENGE NOT YOURSELVES,

but rather

GIVE PLACE UNTO WRATH:

for it is written,

VENGEANCE IS MINE; I WILL REPAY,

saith the Lord.

Therefore

IF THINE ENEMY HUNGER,

FEED HIM;

IF HE THIRST,

GIVE HIM DRINK:

for in so doing thou shalt heap coals of fire on his head.

B-E   N-O-T   O-V-E-R-C-O-M-E   O-F   E-V-I-L,

but

O-V-E-R-C-O-M-E   E-V-I-L   W-I-T-H   G-O-O-D.

(Romans 12:9-21)

Because the foolishness of God is *wiser* than men; and the weakness of God is *stronger* than men. For ye see your calling, brethren, how that not many WISE men after the flesh, not many mighty, not many NOBLE, are called: *But God hath chosen the foolish things of the world to confound the wise; and God hath chosen the weak things of the world to confound the things which are mighty;* **And base things of the world, and things which are *d-e-s-p-i-s-e-d* hath God *c-h-o-s-e-n*, yea, and things which are not, to bring to nought things that are:** THAT NO FLESH (PERSON) SHOULD GLORY (BOAST) IN HIS PRESENCE. But of him are ye in Christ Jesus, who of God is made unto us *wisdom*, and *righteousness*, and *sanctification*, and *redemption*: That, according as

102

it is written, He that glorieth, let him glory in the Lord. (1 Corinthians 1:25-31)

Now in this that I declare unto you **I PRAISE YOU NOT,** that ye come together not for the better, but for the *worse.* For first of all, when ye come together in the church, I hear that there be DIVISIONS among you; and I partly believe it. For there must be also HERESIES among you, that they which are approved may be made manifest among you. When ye come together therefore into one place, this is not to eat the Lord's supper. <u>For in eating every one taketh before other his own supper: and one is hungry, and another is drunken</u>. **WHAT?** have ye not houses to eat and to drink in? *or* **D-E-S-P-I-S-E YE THE CHURCH OF GOD, and SHAME THEM THAT HAVE NOT (THE POOR)?** what shall I say to you? shall I praise you in this? I PRAISE YOU <u>NOT</u>. For I have received of the Lord that which also I delivered unto you, *that the Lord Jesus the same night in which he was betrayed took bread: And when he had given thanks, he brake it, and said, Take, eat: this is my body, which is broken for you: this do in remembrance of me. After the same manner also he took the cup, when he had supped, saying, this cup is the new testament in my blood: this do ye, as oft as ye drink it, in remembrance of me. For as often as ye eat this bread, and drink this cup, ye do shew the Lord's death till he come. **Wherefore WHOSOEVER SHALL EAT THIS BREAD, and DRINK THIS CUP OF THE LORD, U-N-W-O-R-T-H-I-L-Y, SHALL BE GUILTY OF THE BODY and BLOOD OF THE LORD. But let a man <u>EXAMINE HIMSELF</u>, and so let him eat of that bread, and drink of that cup. For he** that eateth and drinketh UNWORTHILY, EATETH and DRINKETH D-A-M-N-A-T-I-O-N TO HIMSELF, not discerning the Lord's body. **For this cause *many* are WEAK and SICKLY among you, and *many* SLEEP.** *For* IF WE WOULD J-U-D-G-E O-U-R-S-E-LV-E-S, WE SHOULD NOT BE JUDGED. ***But*** when we are judged, **WE ARE CHASTENED OF THE LORD, THAT WE SHOULD NOT BE CONDEMNED WITH THE WORLD.** (1 Corinthians 11:17-32)

SUBMITTING YOURSELVES ONE TO ANOTHER IN THE FEAR OF GOD. ***Wives,*** submit yourselves unto your own husbands, as unto the Lord. For the husband is the head of the wife, even as Christ is the head of the church: and he is the saviour of the body. Therefore as the church is subject unto Christ, so let the wives be to their own husbands in every thing. ***Husbands,*** love your wives, *even as Christ also loved the church, and gave himself for it;* That he might sanctify and cleanse it with the washing of water by the word, *That he might present it to himself a glorious church, **not*** having spot, or wrinkle, or any such thing; but that it should be holy and without blemish. **So ought men to love their wives as their own bodies.** He that loveth his wife loveth himself. For no man ever yet **H-A-T-E-D** his own flesh; but nourisheth and cherisheth it, even as the Lord the church: For we are members of his body, of his flesh, and of his bones. For this cause shall a man leave his father and mother, and shall be joined unto his wife, and they two shall be one flesh. ***This is a great mystery: but I speak concerning Christ and the church.*** Nevertheless let every one of you in particular so LOVE HIS WIFE EVEN AS HIMSELF; *and* THE WIFE SEE THAT SHE REVERENCE HER HUSBAND. (Ephesians 5:21-33)

Furthermore then we beseech you, brethren, and exhort you by the Lord Jesus, that as *ye have received of us* **how ye ought to walk and to please God,** *so ye would abound more and more.* For ye know what commandments we gave you by the Lord Jesus. For this is the will of God, even your sanctification, that ye should **ABSTAIN FROM FORNICATION: That every one of you should know how to possess (control) his vessel (body) in sanctification and honour;** *Not* **in the lust of CONCUPISCENCE (strong sinful desires; especially sexually),** even as the Gentiles which know not God: That no man go beyond and defraud his brother in any matter: *because that the Lord is the avenger of all such,* as we also have forewarned you and testified. *For* **GOD HATH NOT CALLED US UNTO UNCLEANNESS,** *but* **UNTO HOLINESS (SINLESS LIVING). HE** *therefore* **THAT D-E-S-P-I-S-E-T-H (THE REQUIREMENT OF SINLESS LIVING), D-E-S-P-I-S-E-T-H NOT M-A-N (THE MEN WHO GIVE THESE INSTRUCTIONS),** *b-u-t* **G-O-D,** who hath also given unto us his holy Spirit. (1 Thessalonians 4:1-8)

Now we exhort you, brethren, **warn them that are UNRULY,** comfort the feebleminded, support the weak, be patient toward all men. **SEE THAT NONE RENDER EVIL FOR EVIL UNTO ANY MAN;** *but* **EVER FOLLOW THAT WHICH IS GOOD,** *both* **AMONG YOURSELVES,** *and* **TO**

ALL MEN. <u>Rejoice evermore.</u> <u>Pray without</u> <u>ceasing.</u> <u>In every thing give thanks:</u> for this is the will of God in Christ Jesus concerning you. Quench not the Spirit. <u>D-E-S-P-I-S-E</u> *not* <u>prophesyings.</u> <u>Prove all things;</u> <u>hold fast that which</u> <u>is good.</u> **ABSTAIN FROM ALL *APPEARANCE* OF EVIL.** (1 Thessalonians 5:14-22)

This know also, that in the last days P-E-R-I-L-O-U-S TIMES shall come. **For men shall be** <u>**LOVERS OF THEIR OWN SELVES,**</u> <u>**COVETOUS, BOASTERS, PROUD,**</u> <u>**BLASPHEMERS, DISOBEDIENT TO**</u> <u>**PARENTS, UNTHANKFUL, UNHOLY,**</u> <u>**WITHOUT NATURAL AFFECTION,**</u> <u>**TRUCEBREAKERS, FALSE ACCUSERS,**</u> <u>**INCONTINENT, FIERCE, DESPISERS OF**</u> <u>**THOSE THAT ARE GOOD, TRAITORS,**</u> <u>**HEADY, HIGHMINDED, LOVERS OF**</u> <u>**PLEASURES MORE THAN LOVERS OF**</u> <u>**GOD;**</u> **Having a form of godliness, *but* denying the power thereof: FROM SUCH T-U-R-N A-W-A-Y-.** (2 Timothy 3:1-5)

Put them in mind to <u>be subject to principalities and</u> <u>powers,</u> <u>to obey magistrates,</u> to be <u>ready to every</u> <u>good work,</u> <u>To speak evil of no man,</u> <u>to be *no*</u> <u>brawlers,</u> *but* <u>gentle,</u> <u>shewing all meekness unto all</u> <u>men.</u> **For we ourselves also *were* sometimes** <u>**FOOLISH, DISOBEDIENT, DECEIVED,**</u> <u>**SERVING DIVERS LUSTS and PLEASURES,**</u> <u>**LIVING IN MALICE and ENVY, H-A-T-E-F-U-L,**</u> and <u>**H-A-T-I-N-G**</u> **ONE ANOTHER.** *B-u-t after that the kindness and love of God our Saviour toward man appeared,* Not by works of righteousness which we have done, *but*

106

ACCORDING TO HIS MERCY he saved us, by the washing of regeneration, and renewing of the Holy Ghost; Which he shed on us abundantly through Jesus Christ our Saviour; That being justified by his grace, *we should be made heirs according to the hope of eternal life.* This is a faithful saying, and these things I will that thou affirm constantly, that they which have believed in God might BE CAREFUL TO MAINTAIN GOOD WORKS. These things are good and profitable unto men. (Titus 3:1-8)

God, who at sundry times and in divers manners spake in time past unto the fathers by the prophets, Hath in these last days spoken unto us by HIS SON, whom he hath appointed heir of all things, by whom also he made the worlds; *Who being the brightness of his glory, and the express image of his person, and upholding all things by the word of his power, when he had by himself purged our sins, sat down on the right hand of the Majesty on high: Being made so much better than the angels, as he hath by inheritance obtained* **_a more excellent name_** *than they.* For unto which of the angels said he at any time, Thou art my Son, this day have I begotten thee? And again, I will be to him a Father, and he shall be to me a Son? And again, when he bringeth in the firstbegotten into the world, he saith, And let all the angels of God worship him. And of the angels he saith, Who maketh his angels spirits, and his ministers a flame of fire. *But* unto the SON he saith, **_Thy throne, O God, is for ever and ever: a sceptre of righteousness is the sceptre of thy kingdom. Thou hast L-O-V-E-D RIGHTEOUSNES, and H-A-T-E-D INIQUITY; therefore God, even thy God, hath anointed thee_** *with the oil of gladness above thy fellows.* And, Thou, Lord, in the beginning hast laid the foundation of the earth; and the heavens are the works of thine hands: They shall perish; but thou remainest; and they all shall wax old as doth a garment; And as a vesture shalt thou fold them up, and they shall be changed: but thou art the same, and thy years shall not fail. But to which of the angels said he at any time, Sit on my right hand, until I make thine enemies thy footstool? *Are they not all **ministering spirits**, sent forth to minister for them who shall be heirs of salvation?* (Hebrews 1:1-14)

HE THAT D-E-S-P-I-S-E-D MOSES' LAW DIED WITHOUT MERCY under two or three witnesses: **OF HOW MUCH S-O-R-E-R P-U-N-I-S-H-M-E-N-T, suppose ye, shall he be thought worthy, WHO HATH TRODDEN UNDER FOOT THE SON OF GOD, and hath counted the blood of the covenant, wherewith he was sanctified, an unholy thing, and hath done despite unto the Spirit of grace?** For we know him that hath said, **VENGEANCE BELONGETH UNTO ME, I WILL RECOMPENSE (REPAY), saith the Lord.** And again, **THE LORD SHALL JUDGE HIS PEOPLE, IT IS A FEARFUL THING TO FALL INTO THE HANDS OF THE LIVING GOD.** (Hebrews 10:28-31)

Wherefore seeing we also are compassed about with so great a cloud of witnesses, LET US LAY ASIDE EVERY WEIGHT, and THE SIN WHICH DOTH SO EASILY BESET US, and LET US RUN WITH PATIENCE THE RACE THAT IS SET BEFORE US, *Looking unto Jesus the author and finisher of our faith; who for the joy that was set before him endured the cross, despising the shame, and is set down at the right hand of the throne of God.* FOR CONSIDER HIM THAT ENDURED SUCH CONTRADICTION OF SINNERS AGAINST HIMSELF, LEST YE BE WEARIED and FAINT IN YOUR MINDS. Ye have not yet resisted unto blood, striving against sin. And ye have forgotten the exhortation which speaketh unto you as unto children, My son,

<u>D-E-S-P-I-S-E</u> N-O-T T-H-O-U T-H-E

C-H-A-S-T-E-N-I-N-G

O-F T-H-E L-O-R-D,

nor

F-A-I-N-T W-H-E-N T-H-O-U A-R-T

R-E-B-U-K-E-D

O-F H-I-M:

For whom the Lord loveth he <u>CHASTENETH</u>, and <u>SCOURGETH</u> every son whom he receiveth. If ye endure <u>CHASTENING</u>, God dealeth with you as with SONS; for what son is he whom the father chasteneth not? B-u-t if ye be withOUT chastisement, whereof all are partakers, then are ye <u>BASTARDS</u>, and not sons. Furthermore we have had fathers of our flesh which corrected us, and we gave them reverence: **shall we not much**

rather be in subjection unto the Father of spirits, and live? For they verily for a few days chastened us after their own pleasure; *but* HE FOR OUR PROFIT, THAT WE MIGHT BE PARTAKERS OF HIS HOLINESS. **Now no chastening for the present seemeth to be joyous, but GRIEVOUS:** *nevertheless afterward it yieldeth the peaceable FRUIT OF RIGHTEOUSNESS unto them which are exercised thereby.* Wherefore lift up the hands which hang down, and the feeble knees; And make straight paths for your feet, lest that which is lame be turned out of the way; *but* let it rather be healed. (Hebrews 12:1-13)

My brethren, have *not* the faith of our Lord Jesus Christ, the Lord of glory, with RESPECT OF PERSONS. For if there come unto your assembly a man with a gold ring, in goodly apparel, and there come in also a poor man in vile raiment; And ye have **respect** to him that weareth the gay clothing, and say unto him, Sit thou here in a good place; and say to the poor, Stand thou there, or sit here under my footstool: ARE YE NOT THEN PARTIAL IN YOURSELVES, and ARE BECOME JUDGES OF EVIL THOUGHTS? Hearken, my beloved brethren, *Hath not God chosen the poor of this world rich in faith, and heirs of the kingdom which he hath promised to them that love him?* **But YE HAVE D-E-S-P-I-S-E-D THE POOR. Do not rich men oppress you, and draw you before the judgment seats? Do not they blaspheme that worthy name by the which ye are called?** If ye fulfil the royal law according to the scripture, *Thou shalt love thy neighbour as thyself, ye do well:* **B-u-t if ye have respect to persons, YE COMMIT SIN, and are convinced of the law as**

transgressors.   For whosoever shall keep the whole law, and yet offend in one point, HE IS GUILTY OF ALL. (James 2:1-10)

The Lord knoweth how to deliver the GODLY out of temptations, **and to reserve the UNJUST unto the day of judgment to be punished:**   But chiefly **them that walk (live) after the <u>flesh</u> in the LUST OF UNCLEANNESS, and <u>DESPISE</u> GOVERNMENT. PRESUMPTUOUS are they, SELFWILLED, they are not afraid to speak evil of dignities.**   Whereas angels, which are greater in power and might, bring not railing accusation against them before the Lord.   **But these, as natural brute beasts, made to be taken and DESTROYED, speak evil of the things that they understand not; and SHALL UTTERLY PERISH IN THEIR OWN CORRUPTION;** *And* **shall receive the REWARD OF UNRIGHTEOUSNESS, as they that count it PLEASURE TO RIOT IN THE DAY TIME.** Spots they are and blemishes, **SPORTING THEMSELVES WITH THEIR OWN <u>DECEIVINGS</u>** while they feast with you; **Having EYES FULL OF ADULTERY, and THAT <u>CANNOT CEASE FROM SIN</u>;** beguiling unstable souls: an heart they have exercised with covetous practices; **<u>CURSED CHILDREN</u>:** Which have **FORSAKEN THE RIGHT WAY,** and are gone astray, following the way of Balaam the son of Bosor, **WHO LOVED THE WAGES OF UNRIGHTEOUSNESS;** *But* was rebuked for his iniquity: the dumb ass speaking with man's voice forbad the madness of the prophet. These are wells without water, clouds that are carried with a tempest; **TO WHOM THE MIST OF**

DARKNESS IS RESERVED FOR EVER. For when they speak great swelling words of vanity, they allure through the **LUSTS OF THE FLESH,** through **MUCH WANTONNESS,** those that were clean escaped from them who **LIVE IN ERROR.** While they promise them liberty, they themselves are the **SERVANTS OF CORRUPTION: for of whom a man is overcome, of the same is he brought in BONDAGE. For if after they have escaped the pollutions of the world through the knowledge of the Lord and Saviour Jesus Christ, they are** *again* **entangled therein, and OVERCOME, THE LATTER END IS WORSE WITH THEM THAN THE BEGINNING. For it had been better for them** *not* **to have known the way of righteousness, than, after they have known it, to TURN from the holy commandment delivered unto them.** *But* **it is happened unto them according to the TRUE PROVERB, THE DOG IS TURNED TO HIS OWN VOMIT AGAIN;** *and* **THE SOW THAT WAS WASHED TO HER WALLOWING IN THE MIRE.** (2 Peter 2:9-22)

He that *saith* he is in the light, *and (but)* **HATETH** his brother, IS IN DARKNESS EVEN UNTIL NOW. *He that LOVETH his brother abideth in the light,* and there is none occasion of stumbling in him. *But* **he that HATETH his brother (brother in Christ) is in darkness, and walketh in darkness, and knoweth not whither he goeth,** *because* **that darkness hath blinded his eyes.** (1 John 2:9-11)

Not as **Cain,** who was of that WICKED ONE, and slew his brother. And wherefore slew he him?

Because **HIS OWN WORKS WERE EVIL, and HIS BROTHER'S RIGHTEOUS. Marvel not, my brethren, IF THE WORLD H-A-T-E YOU.** We know that we have passed from death unto life, *because we love the brethren.* **He that loveth not his brother abideth in death. Whosoever HATETH his brother is a MURDERER: and ye know that NO MURDERER HATH ETERNAL LIFE ABIDING IN HIM.** Hereby perceive we the love of God, because he laid down his life for us: *and* **we ought to lay down our lives for the brethren.** *But* whoso hath this world's good, and seeth his brother have need, and shutteth up his bowels of compassion from him, **how dwelleth the love of God in him?** My little children, **LET US NOT LOVE IN WORD, NEITHER IN TONGUE; but in D-E-E-D and in T-R-U-T-H.** (1 John 3:12-18)

Whosoever shall confess that Jesus is the Son of God, God dwelleth in him, and he in God. And we have known and believed the love that God hath to us. *God is love; and he that dwelleth in love dwelleth in God, and God in him.* Herein is our love made perfect, that *WE MAY HAVE BOLDNESS IN THE DAY OF JUDGMENT: because* as he is, so are we in this world. ***There is no fear in love; but perfect love casteth out fear:*** because fear hath torment. He that feareth is not made perfect in love. *We love him, because he first loved us.* If a man say, I love God, **and HATETH HIS BROTHER, HE IS A LIAR:** for he that loveth not his brother whom he hath seen, how can he love God whom he hath not seen? And this COMMANDMENT have we from him, THAT HE

WHO LOVETH GOD LOVE HIS BROTHER
ALSO. (1 John 4:12-21)

Even as Sodom and Gomorrha, and the cities about
them in like manner, **GIVING THEMSELVES
OVER TO FORNICATION,** *and* **GOING
AFTER STRANGE FLESH, are set forth for an**
example, **SUFFERING THE VENGEANCE OF
ETERNAL FIRE.** *Likewise also* **THESE
FILTHY DREAMERS DEFILE THE FLESH,
DESPISE DOMINION, and SPEAK EVIL OF
DIGNITIES.** Yet Michael the archangel, when
contending with the devil he disputed about the
body of Moses, durst not bring against him a railing
accusation, but said, **THE LORD REBUKE
THEE.** But these speak evil of those things which
they know *not*: but what they know naturally, as
brute beasts, in those things **THEY CORRUPT
THEMSELVES.** (Jude 1:7-10)

Unto the angel of the CHURCH OF EPHESUS
write; These things saith he (Jesus) that holdeth the
SEVEN STARS IN HIS RIGHT HAND, who
walketh in the midst of the SEVEN GOLDEN
CANDLESTICKS; I know thy works, and thy
labour, and thy patience, and how thou canst not
bear them which are evil: and thou hast tried them
which say they are apostles, and are not, and hast
found them liars: And hast borne, and hast
patience, and for my name's sake hast laboured, and
hast not fainted. *N-e-v-e-r-t-h-e-l-e-s-s* **I have
somewhat against thee,** *because* **THOU HAST
LEFT THY FIRST LOVE.** Remember therefore
from whence thou art fallen, and **REPENT,** and DO
THE FIRST WORKs; *or else* **I will come unto thee
quickly, and will remove thy candlestick out of**

114

his place, except thou **REPENT**. *But* this thou hast (in thy favor), that **THOU H-A-T-E-S-T THE DEEDS OF THE NICOLAITANES (INDULGENCE, ESPECIALLY SEXUAL INDULGENCES and EATING FOOD OFFERED TO IDOLS), WHICH I ALSO H-A-T-E.** *He that hath an ear, LET HIM HEAR what the Spirit saith unto the churches;* To him that **O-V-E-R-C-O-M-E-T-H** *will I give to eat of the tree of life, which is in the midst of the paradise of God.* And unto the angel of the CHURCH IN SMYRNA write; These things saith the first and the last, which was dead, and is alive (Jesus); I know thy works, and tribulation, and poverty, **(but thou art rich)** and I know the blasphemy of them which say they are Jews, and are not, but are the synagogue of Satan. FEAR NONE OF THOSE THINGS WHICH THOU SHALT SUFFER: **behold, the devil shall cast some of you into prison, that ye may be tried; and ye shall have TRIBULATION TEN DAYS:** *be thou faithful unto DEATH, and I will give thee a crown of life.* He that hath an ear, LET HIM HEAR what the Spirit saith unto the churches; He that **O-V-E-R-C-O-M-E-T-H** shall not be hurt of the second death. And to the angel of the CHURCH IN PERGAMOS write; These things saith he which hath *the sharp sword with two edges(Jesus);* I know thy works, and where thou dwellest, even **where Satan's seat is:** and thou holdest fast my name, and hast not denied my faith, even in those days wherein ANTIPAS WAS MY FAITHFUL MARTYR, who was slain among you, **where Satan dwelleth.** *B-u-t* **I HAVE A FEW THINGS AGAINST THEE,** *because* **thou hast there them that hold the DOCTRINE OF BALAAM (PAGAN DOCTRINES WOVEN IN**

WITH PURE CHURCH DOCTRINES), who taught Balac to cast a stumblingblock before the children of Israel, to EAT THINGS SACRIFICED UNTO IDOLS, and TO COMMIT FORNICATION. So hast thou *also* **THEM THAT HOLD THE DOCTRINE OF THE NICOLAITANES, WHICH THING I H-A-T-E.** REPENT; *or else* I WILL COME UNTO THEE QUICKLY, and WILL FIGHT AGAINST THEM WITH THE SWORD OF MY MOUTH. *He that hath an ear, LET HIM HEAR what the Spirit saith unto the churches;* To him that **O-V-E-R-C-O-M-E-T-H** will I give to eat of the *hidden manna,* and will give him *a white stone,* and in the stone *a new name* written, which no man knoweth saving he that receiveth it. (Revelation 2:1-17)

And there came one of the seven angels which had the SEVEN VIALS, and talked with me, saying unto me, Come hither; **I WILL SHEW UNTO THEE THE JUDGMENT OF THE GREAT WHORE THAT SITTETH UPON MANY WATERS: WITH WHOM THE KINGS OF THE EARTH HAVE COMMITTED FORNICATION, and THE INHABITANTS OF THE EARTH HAVE BEEN MADE DRUNK WITH THE WINE OF HER FORNICATION.** So he carried me away in the spirit into the wilderness: and **I SAW A WOMAN SIT UPON A *SCARLET* COLOURED BEAST, full of names of blasphemy, having seven heads and ten horns. And the woman was arrayed in PURPLE and SCARLET colour, and decked with GOLD and PRECIOUS STONES and PEARLS, having a GOLDEN CUP in her hand full of abominations** and filthiness of her FORNICATION: And upon her forehead was a name written, **MYSTERY, BABYLON THE GREAT, THE MOTHER OF HARLOTS AND ABOMINATIONS OF THE EARTH.** And I saw the woman <u>drunken with the blood of the saints, and with the blood of the martyrs of Jesus</u>: and when I saw her, I wondered with great admiration. And the angel said unto me, Wherefore didst thou marvel? <u>I will tell thee the mystery of the woman,</u> and of the beast that carrieth her, which hath the <u>seven heads</u> and <u>ten horns</u>. The beast that thou sawest was, and is not; and shall ascend out of the **BOTTOMLESS PIT,** and go into **PERDITION:** and they that dwell on the earth shall wonder, whose names were *not* written in the BOOK OF LIFE from the foundation of the world, when they behold the beast that **was,** *and* **is not,** *and* **yet is.** And here is the mind which hath wisdom. The SEVEN HEADS are SEVEN MOUNTAINS, on which the woman sitteth. And there are SEVEN KINGS: <u>five are fallen</u>, and <u>one is</u>, and <u>the other is not yet come</u>; and when he cometh, he must continue a short space. And the **BEAST** that **was,** and **is not,** even he *is* the eighth, and *is of* the seven, and **GOETH INTO PERDITION.** And the TEN HORNS which thou sawest are TEN KINGS, <u>which have received no kingdom as yet</u>; *but* <u>receive power as kings one hour with the beast</u>. These have **ONE MIND, and SHALL GIVE THEIR POWER and STRENGTH UNTO THE BEAST. THESE SHALL MAKE WAR WITH THE LAMB, and THE LAMB SHALL O-V-E-R-C-O-M-E THEM: FOR HE IS LORD of LORDS, and KING of KINGS:** *and they that are with him are* <u>*called*</u>, *and* <u>*chosen*</u>, *and* <u>*faithful.*</u> And he saith unto me, The WATERS which thou sawest, where the WHORE sitteth, are PEOPLES, and MULTITUDES, and NATIONS, and TONGUES. **And the TEN HORNS which thou sawest upon the beast, these shall H-A-T-E THE WHORE, and shall make her desolate and naked, and shall eat her flesh, and burn her with fire. For God hath put in their hearts to fulfil his will, and to agree, and GIVE THEIR KINGDOM UNTO THE BEAST, until the words of God shall be fulfilled.** *And* THE WOMAN WHICH THOU SAWEST IS THAT GREAT CITY, WHICH REIGNETH OVER THE KINGS OF THE EARTH. (Revelation 17:1-18)

And after these things I saw ANOTHER ANGEL come down from heaven, having great power; and the earth was lightened with his glory. And he cried mightily with a strong voice, saying, **BABYLON THE GREAT IS FALLEN, IS FALLEN, and IS BECOME THE HABITATION OF DEVILS, and THE HOLD OF EVERY FOUL SPIRIT, and A CAGE OF EVERY UNCLEAN and HATEFUL BIRD. For all nations have drunk of the wine of the WRATH of her FORNICATION, and the kings of the earth have committed FORNICATION WITH HER, and the merchants of the earth are waxed rich through the abundance of her delicacies.** And I heard another voice from heaven, saying, **COME OUT OF HER, MY PEOPLE, THAT YE BE NOT PARTAKERS OF HER SINS,** *and* **THAT YE RECEIVE NOT OF HER PLAGUES**. For her sins have reached unto heaven, and God hath remembered her INIQUITIES. **Reward her even as she rewarded**

118

you, and D-O-U-B-L-E unto her D-O-U-B-L-E according to her works: in the cup which she hath filled fill to her   D-O-U-B-L-E. How much she hath glorified herself, and lived deliciously, so much TORMENT and SORROW give her: for she saith in her heart, I sit a queen, and am no widow, and shall see no sorrow. *Therefore* shall her P-L-A-G-U-E-S come in **ONE DAY**, death, and mourning, and famine; and she shall be utterly burned with fire: *for STRONG is the Lord God who judgeth her.* And the KINGS OF THE EARTH, who have committed FORNICATION and lived deliciously with her, shall bewail her, and lament for her, when they shall see the smoke of her burning, Standing afar off for the fear of her torment, saying, ALAS, ALAS THAT GREAT CITY BABYLON, THAT MIGHTY CITY! for IN ONE HOUR IS THY JUDGMENT COME. (Revelation 18:1-10)

www.ingramcontent.com/pod-product-compliance
Lightning Source LLC
Chambersburg PA
CBHW061746020426
42331CB00006B/1375